Potomac Pathway:

A Nature Guide to the C & O Canal

Napier Shelton

4880 Lower Valley Road Atglen, Pennsylvania 19310

Other Schiffer Books on Related Subjects:
Chesapeake Bay, A Field Guide: Nature of the Estuary. Christopher P. White. Drawings by Karen Teramura. ISBN: 9780870333514. $14.99
The Traveling Nature Photographer: A Guide for Exploring the Natural World through Photography. Steven Morello. ISBN: 9780764330551. $29.99

Library of Congress Control Number: 2011925922

Designed by Bruce Waters
Type set in Goudy Oldstyle/Humanist 521 BT

ISBN: 978-0-7643-3798-7
Printed in China

Schiffer Books are available at special discounts for bulk purchases for sales promotions or premiums. Special editions, including personalized covers, corporate imprints, and excerpts can be created in large quantities for special needs. For more information contact the publisher:

Published by Schiffer Publishing Ltd.
4880 Lower Valley Road
Atglen, PA 19310
Phone: (610) 593-1777; Fax: (610) 593-2002
E-mail: Info@schifferbooks.com

For the largest selection of fine reference books on this and related subjects, please visit our website at **www.schifferbooks.com**
We are always looking for people to write books on new and related subjects. If you have an idea for a book please contact us at the above address.

This book may be purchased from the publisher.
Include $5.00 for shipping.
Please try your bookstore first.
You may write for a free catalog.

In Europe, Schiffer books are distributed by
Bushwood Books
6 Marksbury Ave.
Kew Gardens
Surrey TW9 4JF England
Phone: 44 (0) 20 8392 8585; Fax: 44 (0) 20 8392 9876
E-mail: info@bushwoodbooks.co.uk
Website: www.bushwoodbooks.co.uk

Dedication

To Douglas Bruce McHenry and his parents, Donald E. and Bona May McHenry

Acknowledgments

My debt to others goes a long way back. I was introduced to the C & O Canal when I was about six years old, by Donald McHenry, first Chief Park Naturalist of the National Capital Region, his wife Bona May, and their son, my first grade classmate, Bruce McHenry. They lived in the lockhouse at Lock 7, so I learned much about that area, as well as other stretches of the canal near Washington, both from the McHenrys and from members of the Audubon Society of the District of Columbia, later renamed the Audubon Naturalist Society of the Central Atlantic States. In later years I visited all parts of the canal, some many times.

This book had its beginning in the 1970s, when I wrote a manuscript about nature in the C & O Canal National Historical Park for the NPS handbook series. It was not published, however, because the NPS Publications Division decided instead to focus the book on the history of the canal (Handbook 142). In the 1990s, the Publications Division gave me permission to use my manuscript as a basis for a new, considerably revised version, intended to be a privately published guide to natural features people can see along and near the canal.

For help with the first and later versions of the book I am indebted to many people. First and foremost, I thank Connie Durnan, whose photographic and computer assistance made this book possible. The majority of photographs are by her. (Photos without attribution are by the author.) Members of the National Park Service include William Perry, William Justice, Dianne Ingram and Marie Souter (who both read the entire manuscript), Scott Bell, Dale Nisbet, Bob Ford, Sue Salmans, and Ken Ferebee. Specialists with the Maryland Department of Natural Resources also contributed much essential information. Ed Thompson created and reviewed two of the checklists and reviewed other parts of the manuscript. Glen Therres brought me up to date on eagle nesting along the Potomac. Dick Wiegand described outstanding wildflower areas and reviewed parts of the manuscript. Ed Enamait (fisheries), Robert Colona (otters), Steve Bittner (furbearers), and Susan Rivers (Potomac River mayflies) helped with those subjects.

Chandler Robbins added species to my bird checklist and Craig Koppie related the fortunes of the American Legion Bridge peregrines; both men are with the U.S. Fish and Wildlife Service. William Davies (whose identification of specific rock outcrops I have followed in most cases), Robert Sigafoos, Avery Drake, Jr., and C. Scott Southworth, all of the U.S. Geological Survey, provided most of what I know about geology of the Potomac Basin. On an Audubon Naturalist Society trip, Joe Marx explained geological features of the Harpers Ferry area. I also thank Neal Fitzpatrick and Stephanie Mason of the Audubon Naturalist Society for their interest and answers to my questions.

Many others helped in special ways. Bob and Fanny Johnsson showed me unique adaptations of rare plants to habitats at Great Falls and shale barrens in Green Ridge State Forest. Francis Zumbrun, forest manager at Green Ridge State Forest, described the different forms of forest management there. William (Marty) Martin told me about rattlesnakes on South Mountain. Stanwyn Shetler, of the Smithsonian Institution, read an earlier draft. Herbert Harris and George Zug gave me information about reptiles and amphibians, and Jim Greene about the American Legion Bridge peregrines. Milo Meacham introduced me to the mysteries of digital cameras, and Gail Prensky helped with key computer operations. Jim Paulus supplied both information and companionship on the canal back in the 1970s. George and Danielle DuBois offered hospitality and then (George) assistance on regional bird counts in the Big Pool area. My wife, Elizabeth, gamely pushed her bicycle through the mud as we traversed the Williamsport-Hancock section, and pushed me forward with good suggestions when I bogged down in the creation of this book.

My knowledge of the canal came from all these people, those who wrote the publications in Further Reading or developed parts of the Appendix, and from my own 70 years walking or biking the canal towpath. It has been a hugely enjoyable collaboration for which I give thanks.

Contents

Introduction

At 30th Street in Georgetown, beside the Chesapeake and Ohio Canal, a bust of Justice William O. Douglas faces upstream. It gazes up a towpath that runs between the canal and the Potomac River, through flood plain forests of towering sycamore and maple, past fields of grass and corn, through ancient mountain ridges, and finally to its terminus at Cumberland, deep in the Appalachians. It's a peaceful, bucolic route, with an air of wildness. It's for people who walk, and ride horses and bicycles, for canoeists and fishers, photographers and painters, birders and botanizers.

Justice Douglas leads the hike that aroused public support for a C & O Canal National Historical Park. Out of sight are those who couldn't keep up with his rapid pace. *Courtesy of C & O Canal National Historical Park.*

In the 1950s, however, it almost became a route for automobiles. The C & O Canal, never much of a commercial success, ceased operation in 1924 after another in a series of destructive floods. In 1938, the Baltimore and Ohio Railroad, the canal's owner since 1890, sold it to the U.S. Government for $2 million. Government planners proposed turning it into a parkway. This appeared likely until Justice Douglas, in 1954, argued otherwise and organized his now-famous walk from Cumberland to Georgetown, taking along *Washington Post* editors who had supported the parkway idea, as well as conservationists. Minds were changed, and the weight of public sentiment eventually convinced officialdom to scrap the parkway. In 1961 President Eisenhower signed a proclamation establishing the Chesapeake and Ohio Canal National Monument, and in 1971 President Nixon signed the act of Congress changing the canal's status to the more firmly protected Chesapeake and Ohio Canal National Historical Park. The legislation established the park "to preserve and interpret the historic and scenic features of the Chesapeake and Ohio Canal, and to develop the potential of the canal for public recreation...." Canal structures would be maintained or restored, the adjacent land would remain in its natural state, with the exception of some agricultural fields as part of the cultural landscape. As a consequence, the towpath today is a much-loved trail through both history and nature.

The nature, the subject of this book, is rich. Frequently supplied with sediment by the overflowing Potomac, the flood plain supports dense forests of all ages, with a profusion of wildflowers changing with the seasons. A great diversity of animal life—from microorganisms to the occasional black bear—feeds on the plants or each other. Along many parts of the route, the canal traverses higher terraces, with somewhat different biological communities. Here and there the forest is broken with open areas or bluffs, further increasing the variety of habitats and thus of the species that dwell in them. Throughout its length, the canal provides aquatic habitats, from open water to small seeps, swamps (wetlands with woody vegetation), and marshes (wetlands with herbaceous vegetation). The nearby Potomac is home to many waterbirds, fishes, and other riverine creatures, and is a migratory route for birds, from warblers to waterfowl, cormorants, and gulls. A day spent afield along the canal always yields something of special natural history interest.

The following guide, mile by mile, points out where many such things can be seen, things like beaver lodges, heron rookeries, forest succession on old fields, and geological formations. I have, of course, tried to pick features that can be expected to remain in place for some time. Since plants, birds, mammals, and geology are the most easily seen or are of interest to the most people, they receive the lion's share of the treatment. Some points along the way raise questions and invite discussion about environmental health, land use, or the relations of humans to nature. Each mile along the towpath is marked by a milepost. The locations of points of interest are identified to the nearest one-tenth of a mile; many of these fractional distances are estimated. Locations of locks and campsites are included for orientation. Side Trips guide the reader in selected public areas adjacent to the canal. Overviews discuss various subjects from a valley-wide point of view, to put specific sites in a larger context. The Appendix lists plants and animals recorded in or near the national historical park.

The National Park Service reminds visitors that all park resources are protected and must be left in place. More specifically,

It is against federal law to pick, dig, or otherwise collect plants in the park.

Staying on officially marked trails helps prevent damage to and trampling of native vegetation, including rare plants.

Dumping yard waste in parks introduces non-native plants to fragile ecosystems.

For information on lodging and other resources along the canal I recommend Mike High's book, *The C & O Canal Companion*, updated edition, 2000. For updates of his listings visit the **River and Canal Website** at: www.press.jhu.edu/press/ books/potomac-canal.html. Click on **Resources.** His book, published by Johns Hopkins University Press, should be available in any of the National Park Service visitor centers along the canal.

Georgetown to Harpers Ferry

This is one of the most scenic, dramatic sections of the canal's entire 184.5 miles. At Key Bridge the urban environment of Georgetown ends and nature gains ascendancy. Flood plain forest appears on the river side of the canal and then widens. Above Chain Bridge the tidal Potomac ends at Little Falls; upstream it is a succession of riffles and rapids all the way to Violettes Lock at Mile 22. The canal winds through the Potomac River gorge, becoming lake-like at Widewater and passing near tumultuous Great Falls.

Back at Angler's Inn, Mile 12.3, one leaves behind first the traffic on Canal Road, beginning at Key Bridge, and then, from Chain Bridge, Clara Barton Parkway, followed by MacArthur Boulevard, which have paralleled the canal and, with a few departures from earshot, somewhat detracted from the enjoyment of nature. Now, natural sounds dominate most of the way to Cumberland. At Violettes Lock, the remains of Dam No. 2 form a break between rapids below and a broad, quiet Potomac above. The canal is normally watered from Georgetown to Violettes Lock.

Mile 0.3 – The canal begins (or ends) here where it empties into Rock Creek. (Mile 0 is at the tidewater lock, immediately downriver from Thompson's Boat Center.)

Mile 0.4 – The small **National Park Service Georgetown Visitor Center** sells C & O Canal literature and other items, provides information, and arranges interpretive trips—with interpreters in period dress on a mule-drawn barge— which begin near here. The center is open seasonally Wednesday to Sunday, 9:00-4:30. At 30th Street stands the bust of Justice Douglas. Locks 1 through 4 are clustered in the first 1/10 mile of the canal. From Georgetown to Cumberland the elevation rises 604 feet and 74 locks accordingly raised or lowered the water level in the canal for boats traveling upstream or down.

Mile 0.3-1.0 – Commercial and residential buildings line the canal, but bits of nature intrude even here. Tree of Heaven (ailanthus), princess tree, sycamore, and other woody plants sprout from walls. Mallards swim in the canal. Barn and rough-winged swallows nest on or in structures in summer.

Mile 1.0 – The landscape opens up here, with forest on the river side (and boathouses on the Potomac shore).

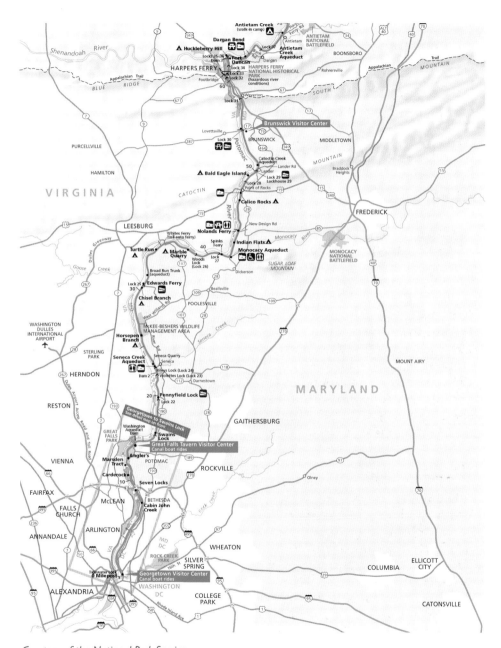

Courtesy of the National Park Service.

Mile 1.5 – Where a spillway from the canal enters the Potomac, ducks, great blue herons, and kingfishers often can be seen. Out in the river, from spring to fall, black, long-necked double-crested cormorants perch and dry their wings on the rocky Three Sisters Islands. They begin arriving in March, when the spring run of herring, shad, and other fish begins. Any time of year you may see Canada geese and gulls here, herring and great black-backed gulls mainly in winter, ring-billed gull fall to spring. Many ring-bills migrate upriver in spring, along with Bonaparte's gulls. Bald eagles could be sighted here as well. There's an eagle nest, probably built in 2008, across the river and slightly upstream, high in a tree amazingly between the east- and west-moving lanes of the busy George Washington Parkway. Eagles in the Washington area usually have eggs by mid- to late-February. With binoculars you can often spot the white head of a brooding eagle.

People in kayaks, canoes, and shells, coming from boathouses near Key Bridge, frequent this stretch of river.

You may get a whiff of sewer smell here. This most likely comes from a vent in the sewer coming down through Glover-Archbold Park or in the Potomac Interceptor, the sewer line running from Dulles Airport to the Blue Plains Treatment Plant. The formerly combined sewers west of Rock Creek Park, which carried both sewage and runoff, have been separated, preventing them from sending sewage into the Potomac during high runoff. A large pipe that carries storm water through Glover-Archbold Park to the river near here parallels the sewage drain, which connects with the Potomac Interceptor. East of Rock Creek Park much separation of combined sewers remains to be accomplished.

Mile 2.2 – The **flood-plain forest** begins to broaden. As is typical along the entire canal, silver maple, sycamore, box elder, green ash, and elms are common, but here you also can see such southern species as willow oak and sweetgum, which drop out farther upriver. This kind of forest has many vines, especially Virginia creeper, poison ivy, and grape, the latter of which can be as thick across as your arm. (See Overview: Flood Plain Trees.)

Mile 3.2 – Fletcher's Cove and Boathouse, where rowboats, canoes, and kayaks can be rented, has been for years a magnet for anglers, especially during spring spawning runs of herring, shad, white perch, and rockfish. As Ray Fletcher, who works for the current concessionaire, Guest Services, explains, weather can cause some variation in arrival times from year to year. Herring, which come from the ocean, normally arrive around April 1 to 5; hickory shad and American shad both come from the ocean, the hickory arriving around April 15, the American May 1-15; white perch arrive from Chesapeake Bay around April 15; rockfish, which have wintered in Chesapeake Bay or the ocean, follow the herring and prey on them, but some may arrive in early March. For up-to-date conditions and fishing information call 202-244-0461 or try www.fletcherscove.com

Park service archeological excavations begun in 1997-98 near the boathouse unearthed about 60,000 artifacts, mostly from the Middle Woodland period, but some from the earlier Archaic; the occupants probably were attracted partly by the seasonally abundant fish. This is also a good birdwatching area, with open patches in the forest, mudflats at low tide, and the river to scan. Wild turkeys are sometimes seen, and deer frequently. The mudflats are partly due to sludge discharged through a pipe from the Dalecarlia water treatment plant to the river above Chain Bridge.

Mile 4.5 – A concrete track extends to the river below Little Falls, a popular spot for fishing in spring. While watching present-day anglers, one can easily imagine Native Americans spearing or netting fish here in this still wild-looking landscape.

The track traverses a wide band of rocky land with small trees bent downstream, which are all that can survive the frequent floods that rage through here. But nearer the canal, where flooding is less frequent and water speed at those times is less, the trees are taller. This is quite evident from Chain Bridge.

Mile 4.8 – Little Falls Branch, which flows from Bethesda along its own parkway, goes under the canal through a concrete culvert.

Mile 5.1 – Lock 5 and **guard lock**. From here to Lock 6 (Mile 5.4), you pass on the river side an area of ponds and forest, a good place for beavers and, in summer, bright yellow prothonotary warblers. Several unofficial "social" trails, as the park service calls them, lace through these woods, including one along the inlet channel from Dam No. 1 that formerly entered the canal through the guard lock but now mostly spills back into the river. Mallards and black ducks frequent this channel in winter.

Mile 5.4 – Lock 6.

Mile 5.7 – The rock rubble of curving **Little Falls Dam** (Dam No. 1) is what remains of a five-foot-high dam built to divert water into the canal. Upriver are five more such dams, including two high ones that also produce electricity; the rest are just remnants like Dam No. 1.

Just upstream is a low, straight dam built in 1959 to divert some of the water for Washington, through the Little Falls Pumping Station. The District of Columbia gets its entire **water supply** from the Potomac, here and at the Washington Aqueduct Dam above Great Falls. It is sent to the Dalecarlia Reservoir, just inside the D.C. on MacArthur Boulevard, where sediment settles, and then to the adjacent Dalecarlia Treatment Plant. From there it is distributed throughout the city. The District has an agreement to get water from the Jennings Randolph Reservoir, on the North Branch of the Potomac above Cumberland, if the flow of the Potomac at Little Falls drops below 360 MGD (million gallons per day). This has not happened since the 1960s. The whole Washington Metropolitan Area gets 85-90 percent of its water from the Potomac, the rest from several local reservoirs.

Near the Virginia shore, a fishway in this dam, completed in 2000 by the U.S. Army Corps of Engineers and the Maryland Department of Natural Resources, enables fish to continue upstream into ten more miles of spawning areas. It slows the current so fish like shad can get up it. An interpretive sign just downstream from the pumping station describes this.

From late fall to early spring, ducks—such as mallards, common mergansers, buffleheads, and ring-necked ducks—feed at Dam No. 1 or in the swift water below it. Kayakers practice slalom runs down the inlet channel.

Mile 6.2 – An **eagle nest** on the Virginia shore can be seen well in leafless seasons. It was formerly behind a dead tree just a few yards upstream from the white buoys in the river warning boaters about the intake dam downstream. The nest had young in March 2007. Later, eagles built a new nest about 200 yards downstream from the former site, in a sycamore at the river's edge, in front of a white house up the hill, from which there must be a good view of eagle domesticity. This is one of at least nine eagle nests between Georgetown and Harpers Ferry.

Mile 6.4 – A rope-guided ferry takes members to the **Montgomery Sycamore Island Club**, founded in 1885 and "dedicated to the preservation and enjoyment of the Potomac River." This is the endpoint of the Potomac River Whitewater Race, held each year in early May.

Mile 6.5 – A small stream tumbles down rock ledges of schist and gneiss to the canal.

Lockhouse 7, home of the McHenry family and meeting place of conservationists.
Photo by Connie Durnan.

Mile 7.0 – Lock 7. During the 1930s and 1940s, **Donald McHenry**, first Chief Park Naturalist for the National Capital Parks, lived in the lockhouse here with his family. A large weeping willow and a sycamore hung over the lock; a chicken house stood just downstream from the lockhouse and a vegetable garden was planted in the dry (after the 1942 flood) canal bed on the upstream side. A jungly forest covered the hill leading up to the Glen Echo amusement park. Naturalists and conservationists, including the ornithologist Roger Tory Peterson, often stopped to visit with the McHenrys and discuss the issues of the day. In 1942 the McHenrys learned firsthand about a frequent problem of lockkeepers—flood. When word came that the river was rising, they moved their furniture upstairs, staked their goats on high ground, anchored the chicken house, and moved to a friend's place. Afterwards, they cleaned out the mud and resumed their life. No one lives in the lockhouse now, though it is well maintained. Donald's son, Bruce, and I spent many happy days roaming this section of the canal.

Mile 7.1-7.5 – On the river side lies 19-acre **Cabin John Island**. Breeding bird censuses conducted here for many years recorded twenty-five or more species each year, but, as in studies in Rock Creek Park and Glover-Archbold Park, some of the birds that winter in the tropics, such as red-eyed vireo, northern parula, American redstart, hooded and Kentucky warblers, and wood thrush, declined precipitously or disappeared. Plenty of birds remain, however, among them the permanent resident species, like Carolina chickadees and cardinals, and in the river channels kingfishers, great blue and green herons, and wood ducks—typical water birds of the Potomac.

Mile 7.3 – For about 100 yards, trees on the berm (the side of the canal opposite the river) are covered with English ivy, and a few with wintercreeper, an Asian Euonymus with drooping branches and elliptical leaves. These evergreen vines are **exotic species**—non-native—that have spread from plantings around houses and thus are most often seen near settlements along the canal. Birds, especially robins and starlings, eat the berries and distribute the seeds in droppings. Exotic plants are a big problem in the C & O Canal National Historical Park and elsewhere, because many of them crowd out native species. Japanese stiltgrass, lesser celandine, and garlic mustard are some of the worst herbaceous offenders along the canal. Non-native trees include ailanthus (tree of heaven), paulownia (princess tree), and paper and white mulberry. (The red mulberry is a native.)

Mile 7.5 – Cabin John Creek flows under the canal. Beginning near Rockville, much of its watershed is protected by Cabin John Regional Park.

Mile 8.4 – The lockhouse at Lock 8 has been restored and has become the **Lockhouse 8 River Center**. Sponsored by the Potomac Conservancy and the National Park Service, it offers opportunities to learn about the canal, the Potomac River, and the Conservancy's work to protect the lands and waters. Recent activities have included bird, wildflower, and dragonfly walks, river storytelling, and hardwood seed collecting for planting in other areas. See its website, www.potomac.org, for current activities. The Nature Conservancy (a separate organization) describes the 15-mile gorge from Great Falls to Theodore

Roosevelt Island as "one of the most ecologically significant natural areas in the entire National Park System," with "one of the highest concentrations of globally rare natural communities in the nation." (See Side Trip: Great Falls)

Mile 8.7-9.5 – Locks 9 through 14.

Mile 8.9 – Just a few yards short of Lock 11, a trail leads to **Plummers Island**, the home of the (still very active) Washington Biologists' Field Club since 1901. The island was given to the U.S. Government in 1959 and now is part of the national historical park. It has been described as "the most thoroughly studied island in North America." The trail to it crosses an excellent area for spring wildflowers, such as yellow trout-lily, spring beauty, cut-leaved toothwort, Virginia bluebells, and sessile trillium, as well as the less common twinleaf, harbinger-of-spring, golden Alexanders, and Coville's phacelia.

There are many other good areas for spring wildflowers along the canal from Glen Echo (Mile 7) to Violettes Lock (Mile 22).

Mile 9.1 – A stand of tall, slender tulip trees on the river side suggests there was once a field here, an environment favorable to germination and growth of this species.

Mile 9.4 – In the summer of 2006, a pair of adult **peregrine falcons** was seen carrying prey to the American Legion Bridge on the Beltway (I-495), indicating a nest. Craig Koppie, a peregrine specialist with the U. S. Fish and Wildlife Service began monitoring and placing nest boxes for the peregrines in 2007. The bridge was painted that year and "screwed things up for the peregrines," he said. Koppie put a nest tray on top of an anchor pier (bridge-supporting pillar). The peregrines laid eggs next to it. He then placed a nest box facing upriver and somebody kicked it into the river. No young were produced that year.

In February 2008, Koppie was lowered in a cherry picker bucket to an anchor pier where he placed a nest box facing downriver and left a dead pigeon. The peregrines used the box and produced three young. Koppie captured the young and both parents in a mist net and banded the young. The adults had already been banded, the female in New York State and the male in Pennsylvania.

In 2009, one young was produced but three eggs were addled.

I saw a peregrine at the nest box on March 10, 2010, but Koppie had not yet checked it for reproduction.

He said the peregrine population has been increasing in the Maryland-Virginia-West Virginia-Delaware region since the 1980s. In 2010 there were 18 nests in Maryland alone.

The restoration of peregrines in the eastern U.S. has seen many of them using human structures such as buildings and bridges for nesting, unlike their former reliance on cliffs. The National Park Service, for the restoration of peregrines, has placed the "hack boxes," where young are raised and released, at cliffs. This includes efforts at Shenandoah National Park and Harpers Ferry National Historical Park (see Mile 60.7). Wherever peregrines decide to nest, it's a great joy to see them back after the end of the DDT days.

Mile 9.9 – The east end of Section C of the **Billy Goat Trail** enters the towpath. There are three sections of the Billy Goat Trail, which runs near the river between here and Mile 13.8. Parts of it are rough and rocky, especially the section farthest upstream (Section A), and require some scrambling.

Mile 10.3 – High above the river, in winter you get a good view of Stubblefield Falls, a long rapid.

Mile 10.4 – A **beaver lodge** formerly on the opposite bank was seen to have two (underwater) entrances when the canal was temporarily drained. Beavers also use bank dens with no lodge over them, and lodges surrounded by water. They move when food supplies diminish or water levels are insufficient. Although beaver signs are frequent along the canal, the animals themselves are infrequently seen, preferring to work at night.

A few willow oaks, a southern species, grow on the berm, and, in the woods hereabout, scattered American hollies.

Mile 10.9 – The west end of Section C of the Billy Goat Trail emerges. Nearby cliffs along the Potomac at **Carderock** are favorite climbing spots.

A beaver lodge, with food sticks in the water.

Mile 11.3 – East end of Section B of the Billy Goat Trail. Note the **beaver lodge** on the berm, with food sticks in the water in front of it for winter use.

Mile 12.2 – West end of Section B of the Billy Goat Trail.

Mile 12.3 – Access to **Angler's Inn**, on MacArthur Boulevard, and to a river put-in point.

An alternative to the towpath around Widewater, just upstream, is a berm road (called the Berma Road by the park service folks at Great Falls), so-called because it is on the berm hillside looking down at Widewater. Enter it from the parking lot adjacent to MacArthur Blvd.

Widewater, one of three lake-like parts of the canal.

Great Falls, with a great blue heron flying across. *Photo by Connie Durnan.*

Mile 12.6-13.5 – This lake-like, rock-rimmed section of the canal, known as **Widewater**, is a former river channel that was left high and dry when the Potomac cut its main channel deeper during the Pleistocene. Red cedars and Virginia pines atop the rocks give it an Oriental look. Statuesque great blue herons sometimes standing on the rocks add to this effect. The rocks along the towpath are primarily mica schist, with outcrops of metagraywacke at, for instance, Miles 12.9 and 13.4. **Mica schist** is a metamorphic rock containing abundant coarse flakes of mica. It was originally shale or mudstone before being transformed by heat and pressure deep within the earth's crust. **Metagraywacke** is a metamorphic rock composed of fine-grained quartz, feldspar, and some mica. It was originally muddy sandstone. These two types of rock, about 500 million years old, form most of the bedrock around Great Falls.

Mile 12.7 – East end of the Billy Goat Trail, Section A. This part of the trail gives a good view of dramatic **Mather Gorge**, once a nesting place for peregrine falcons and now a popular rock-climbing area. Kayakers love to play in the giant standing waves below Great Falls. Hikers on the trail should wear sturdy boots and be prepared for some scrambling over rock outcrops. No pets are allowed on this section of the Billy Goat Trail. Between Miles 12.7 and 13.8 is Bear Island, jointly owned by the National Park Service and The Nature Conservancy.

Miles 13.6-14.4 – Locks 15-20 raise the canal 50 feet past Great Falls.

Mile 13.8 – West end of the Billy Goat Trail, Section A.

A pothole formed by swirling pebbles when this spot was on the river bottom.
Photo by Connie Durnan.

Mather Gorge, formed by rapid downcutting during the Pleistocene.
Photo by Connie Durnan.

Mile 14.1 – A well-maintained boardwalk leads across Olmsted Island to a view of **Great Falls**. Great blue and black-crowned night herons sometimes fish below the falls, and black and turkey vultures often soar overhead. Along the trail you can see potholes in the rock formed by pebbles on the bottom of the river when it flowed at this level. Rapid cutting along a fault line during the Pleistocene, when sea level was much lower and precipitation much greater, formed the Mather Gorge and left Olmsted and some other islands below Great Falls well above the river at normal flows. Recent research suggests that the gorge was formed over the last 35,000 years, representing a very rapid rate of erosion. (See Side Trip: Great Falls and the Potomac Gorge for a discussion of the botany of this unique area.)

Mile 14.4 – Great Falls Tavern, an enlargement of the lockhouse finished in 1831, is now a park service visitor center, with exhibits on canal history and publications for sale. One-hour mule-drawn barge trips are conducted May to October through adjacent Lock 20 and upstream. Interpreters in nineteenth century dress explain lock operation and describe canal life in those days. Funds were provided by Friends of Great Falls Tavern and other organizations to replace the old, no longer seaworthy boat and resume the interpretive trips.

One of the Conn Island eagles takes flight. *Photo by Connie Durnan.*

Many great blue herons nest on Conn Island, along with an eagle pair.
Photo by Connie Durnan.

A concrete platform overlooks the dam that diverts water to the Washington Aqueduct intake, source of a large percentage of the city's water supply. From this platform or the blue-blazed River Trail along the shore you can see **Conn Island**, where **bald eagles** have nested successfully most years since 1986. Their bulky nest was in a large sycamore about halfway up the shore of the island; in 2009, the eagles built a new one near the downstream end of the island. They lay eggs in February or early March, and the young normally fly sometime in June. The eagles apparently are not a concern for the many great blue herons, and a few double-crested cormorants and black-crowned night herons, that nest in trees farther up the island. Many ducks—especially ring-necked ducks—hang around Conn Island from late fall to early spring.

The recovery of bald eagles since the banning of DDT use in 1972 seems to be continuing along the upper Potomac. Nests at Mile 1.5, Mile 6.2, and Mile 18.2 are recent additions to those at Conn Island, Mile 21.7, Mile 29, Whites Ferry, near Nolands Ferry, and Harpers Ferry. There is at least one nest, and probably others, upstream from Harpers Ferry. It will be interesting to see if nesting of ospreys also occurs upstream from tidewater Potomac, where it is common.

Great blue herons begin laying eggs in mid-March. They hatch about one month later, and the young begin flying in mid-June. The squawks and clatter of young in the nest, which can extend into July, may be audible from the trail opposite, along the Maryland shore. After the nesting season, great blues are more dispersed along the river, with numbers generally decreasing with distance above tidewater. Only solid ice sends them all down to unfrozen parts.

Double-crested cormorants have joined the herons nesting on Conn Island.
Photo by Connie Durnan.

Double-crested cormorants are large black birds with long snaky necks that dive for fish. They breed along the Atlantic and Pacific coasts and in mid-central parts of North America. They were not found nesting in Maryland until 1990, but subsequently expanded their breeding in the state, including along the Potomac. It is likely that colonies in addition to the one on Conn Island will become established on the upper Potomac.

Black-crowned night herons are dapper-looking birds with black crowns, black and smooth gray upperparts and light underparts. They tend to nest lower in trees than great blue herons do. Conn Island may be their only nesting site on the upper Potomac, although wild birds have nested at the National Zoo in Washington for years.

Canada geese are plentiful year-round here as along most of the river to Cumberland and perhaps beyond. At Great Falls Tavern they graze the grass to the ground. This subspecies—the once nearly extinct greater Canada goose—was restored to the Midwestern United States as a breeding bird so successfully that Canada geese became a pest on golf courses and elsewhere, and throughout the Northeast as well. Where not hunted, they become quite tame. In early spring the Canada pairs along the Potomac noisily proclaim their appropriation of islands for nesting and chase other geese away. They walk their goslings to grazing areas, including grass at the David Taylor Naval Research Center, where a sign on the Clara Barton Parkway says, "Goose Crossing."

Mile 15.9 – A small pumping station supplies part of Rockville's water.

Pileated Woodpecker

This large black and white woodpecker with a long red crest is common along the canal from Washington to Cumberland. The annual Seneca, Maryland, Christmas Bird Count (CBC), which includes the canal from about Miles 12 to 31, records one of the highest counts of pileated woodpeckers on U.S. CBCs. This bird prefers extensive, mature forests, where it chisels holes to feed on carpenter ants and strips bark to reach wood-boring beetles. A versatile bird, it often works low on trees or on logs, and sometimes digs into anthills. Not restricted to insect food, it also eats such things as acorns, sumac seeds, and poison ivy berries. In Audubon's portrayal of the species, four are posed beside clusters of wild grapes, which perhaps they have been consuming, though one is flying off with a grub. Very early in spring, nest excavation begins within a large, sometimes elliptical entrance hole. If you hear a loud, yelping "cuk cuk cuk," it's probably a pileated charging through the forest.

Mile 16.1 – Bamboos line the berm. Clumps of this exotic Asian plant occur at several places along the canal. Sprouting from underground rhizomes, it's difficult to kill but fortunately does not spread very fast.

Mile 16.7 – Swains Lock (No. 21). The Swain family, which lived here, sold refreshments seasonally and rented boats, activities continued today. Several campsites are available beside the river at the Swains Lock Hiker-Biker campground.

Mile 16.9 – More than 130 trees on the berm slope were cut in 2004 and new ones planted within protective tubes. Dan Snyder, owner of the Washington Redskins and the mansion at the top of the hill, cut the trees to improve his view, stating that they were exotic species or diseased trees, and planted small natives. This was controversial because the cut area, though not part of the national historical park, was under scenic easement. Some erosion ensued on the slope. In 2009 beavers crawled up the steep slope and "legally" cut down several more trees for Mr. Snyder. Elsewhere, homeowners have occasionally cut trees on park land to improve their view, and faced penalties.

Mile 17.5 – Watts Branch crosses under the canal. Its watershed reaches to Rockville, and much of the stream flows through residential areas, all of which results in heavy runoff. The Montgomery County Department of Environmental Protection in the late 1980s rated its condition as only "fair," although some 25 species of fish, including smallmouth bass, were found in its lower section, where there is less development.

Nearby, a Washington Suburban Sanitary Commission plant draws water from the Potomac. It is part of a system that supplies Montgomery and Prince George's counties. Overlooking a river channel, plaques with information about the Potomac valley, and benches, make a good rest stop.

Mile 18.2 – In recent years, there were 15 to 30 **great blue heron nests** on a small island just offshore from Watkins Island, though only ten were visible in April 2006 and seven in March 2007. In March 2010 no nests could be seen.

Walkers along the canal often see great blue herons stalking prey in the shallows. Near Washington, this ordinarily wary bird seems unconcerned about people, perhaps because they're so used to them. One can stop and enjoy their ever-so-slow steps, intent pause, and sudden stab at some unfortunate fish or frog. Surveys showed that great blues have steadily increased in Maryland in recent decades, an increase that's apparent along the Potomac.

There's an **eagle's nest** on Watkins Island near the former heron colony site. During winter nest-improvement time, before the herons came back, an observer saw one of the eagles take a stick from a heron nest for use in its own nest. This eagle nest is most visible from about 100 yards upstream from Mile 18, especially when trees are not in leaf.

Mile 19.6 – Lock 22 (Pennyfield Lock). Grover Cleveland, who liked to fish here, stayed at the Pennyfields' frame house that stood on the berm side. It fell into disrepair and has now been removed.

The canal from Pennyfield to Violettes Lock (Mile 22) is a favorite birdwatching area, especially in spring, when warblers and other migrants can be numerous.

Mile 19.8 – Muddy Branch, which passes under the canal here, rises in the Gaithersburg area. Development decreases and condition improves downstream; much of the stream valley has been purchased by Montgomery County for parkland. The flood plain of the middle and lower sections supports a rich spring wildflower community. The warm-water fish community includes abundant bluntnose minnows, swallowtail shiners, and redbreast sunfish.

Mile 20 – The 30-acre **Marshall Dierssen Waterfowl Sanctuary**, managed by the Maryland Department of Natural Resources, extends upstream for about 1 mile between the canal and river. Its two marshy ponds often have ducks, particularly in late fall and early spring. In late summer, shorebirds, such as solitary sandpipers, and egrets and other herons are frequent here.

A large **beaver lodge** sits in the normally swampy upper end of the second pond. However, in October 2007, after a long drought, both ponds were dry and the beaver occupants presumably dwelled elsewhere. As here, things don't always work out the way beavers expect. One often sees along the canal big, or even smaller, trees that beavers have partly or entirely girdled and then for some reason abandoned without felling them, which is evident from the grayed rather than freshly chewed wood. Did they just get tired or bored with those particular trees? Sometimes beavers cut trees that hang up in other trees; they don't control the direction of fall. Though they are said to prefer the bark of cottonwood, aspen, and poplar, trees cut along the canal also include ash, black cherry, box elder, sycamore, hackberry, red oak, Virginia pine, and probably others.

Mile 21.2 – Red cedars adorn the impressive cliffs, formed by gray-green Wissahickon schist, at **Blockhouse Point**, which overlooks a long string of rocky rapids in the river. This is a very scenic section, with the river immediately adjacent to the towpath and high wooded hills on the berm. The canal here is also a favorite fishing place, with large-mouth and smallmouth bass, bluegills, and crappies. The inlet channel at Mile 22 allows frequent influx of fish from the river and under the guard lock gate. Inland from the cliffs is **Blockhouse Point Park**, whose trails can be accessed from River Road.

A turkey vulture suns in a vulture roosting area. *Photo by Connie Durnan*.

Mile 21.5 – Turkey vultures and black vultures often roost in this area on the hillside.

Mile 21.7 – Across the river from approximately this point, there's an **eagle's nest** in a dead tree on a wooded island. It's not visible from here when leaves are out but can be seen from the river shore just above Dam No. 2, ahead. Look with binoculars about a half mile downstream from the dam. This nest was spotted from the air in 2002 and 2004 on DNR flights. It represented a resumption of nesting in this area after an absence of some 40 years and appeared to be still active in 2010. A few great blue herons and cormorants nest a couple hundred yards upstream from the eagles. There must be some reason why eagles and great blues on the Potomac often nest near each other. Perhaps they both like the relative inaccessibility of these sites and an abundance of fish. Or perhaps there's some mutual advantage in the close nesting.

Mile 22 – Lock 23 (Violettes Lock). The remains of Dam No. 2 direct water through a guard lock to the canal. Below the dam the **Seneca Breaks rapids** extend for about a mile. These are shallow most of the year. Most canoeists and kayakers prefer to paddle across the river above the dam and come down through a swift channel on the Virginia side. If just interested in this whitewater run, they then cross the river, take out at Mile 21, and paddle back up the canal if it's watered. (See the chapter, Back by Canoe or Kayak.)

Violettes Lock is a good place to see orioles and yellow-throated warblers; the warblers are partial to sycamores along stream valleys. From fall to spring, look for loons, grebes, waterfowl, and gulls in the river. Except for a few short stretches, the canal is not watered above Violettes Lock.

In spring and late summer this area is rich in wildflowers.

Above Violettes Lock, to Point of Rocks, the canal traverses lowland and the river flows slowly. Away from the riverine forests are many farms. At Point of Rocks, the canal and river cut through Catoctin Mountain, then the Middletown Valley, next, South Mountain followed by the Blue Ridge. It is an engaging succession of pastoral country, woods, and mountains. Except for Brunswick, few signs of urbanity are encountered. One can expect to find occasional ravens, a bird of the mountains, from Point of Rocks on. Geologically, the route traverses both the youngest rock of the upper Potomac (Triassic) and the oldest (Precambrian). The gorge at Harpers Ferry rivals the scenic power of Great Falls.

Mile 22.7 – Lock 24 (Rileys Lock). **Great Seneca Creek** reaches the Potomac under an aqueduct that carries the canal across it. With headwaters near Damascus in northern Montgomery County, the creek passes through Seneca Creek State Park on its way to the river. Little Seneca Creek, a tributary, was dammed to form Little Seneca Lake, the centerpiece of Black Hill Regional Park. Parkland and generally low development density help to maintain Great Seneca Creek in "good" condition.

About 1 mile north of Rileys Lock, where River Road crosses Great Seneca Creek, is Poole's General Store, a genuine country store with well-worn wood floors. It's a good place to pick up a drink and sandwich and marvel at the deer head mounted on the wall. This was the "nontypical" Maryland state champion until 2006. Its peculiar, many-branching antlers have 26 points and received a score of 228 4/8. Jack Poole, son of Raymond and Billie Poole, the lessees of the State-owned historic building, shot the deer on private land just behind his parents' nearby home.

Mile 22.8 – The former **turning basin** is now a pond attractive to painted and the larger red-bellied turtles and various frogs, along with tree swallows, herons, wood ducks, prothonotary warblers, and other birds. Nest boxes for the warblers, cavity-nesters at southern swamps and streams, have been erected along the towpath edge of the pond.

This bird gives its name to an organization—the Prothonotary Society—that is interested in the Whittaker Chambers-Alger Hiss case of the 1930s. These men were Communists involved in passing State Department papers to the Russians. Congressional hearings spent much time investigating whether there was a relationship between the two men. In his book, *Witness*, Chambers explains the role the prothonotary warbler played in proving that relationship:

The point of passing importance was that about the prothonotary warbler, a bird little bigger than a half-dollar [actually 5 1/2 inches long] whose name many people hesitate to pronounce, and which I have never seen. It was that beautiful bird, glimpsed [by Hiss, an avid birdwatcher, and mentioned to Chambers] in a moment of wonder, one summer morning some fourteen years before, that first clinched the Committee's conviction that I must have known Alger Hiss. A mind might figure out … how I might have known the answers to the other questions. But not the prothonotary warbler.

Some years ago I (the author) guided members of the Prothonotary Society to this turning basin on the canal to see their namesake bird.

Much of the canal bed is now full of trees. *Photo by Connie Durnan*.

Mile 23.3 – Bluffs of red sandstone, with narrow bands of shale, begin here and extend for about a half mile before turning inland. Six major quarries in the area supplied sandstone for canal structures from the Seneca Aqueduct to Point of Rocks, as well as for the Smithsonian "castle" and Cabin John Bridge on MacArthur Boulevard. Stone for these last two structures, as well as stone from quarries elsewhere, was cut at the Seneca Stone Cutting Mill, whose ruins lie in woods at the far side of the pond mentioned above.

The sandstone bluffs border a lowland partly occupied by the **McKee-Beshers Wildlife Management Area** (see Side Trip) and reappear along the canal at Mile 30.3. They are part of a lowland trough that extends from Pennsylvania through Maryland into Virginia. Bounded by fault zones (where the earth's crust cracked) on the east and west, the rocks of this lowland are a block of the crust that dropped. The sandstones and some other rocks of this trough are considerably younger (Triassic) than those that bound it, such as the ancient schists and metagraywacke at Great Falls and the slates and basement rock at Point of Rocks, all of which are Cambrian or Precambrian in age.

Mile 24.6 – A few **great blue herons** were nesting on the downstream end of Sharpshin Island, directly offshore, in 2004. Double-crested cormorants appeared to have joined them.

Mile 25.5 – Cornfields of the McKee-Beshers Wildlife Management Area are visible through trees on the berm. Crops are planted on the WMA for wildlife.

Mile 26 – Horsepen Branch Hiker-Biker. A "social" trail crosses the dry canal bed and leads to tracks in the wildlife management area.

Mile 27.2 – Parking lot at the end of Sycamore Landing Road, which enters McKee-Beshers from River Road. This is a good place from which to observe the courtship flights of woodcocks in March around dusk. The canal parkland in either direction is good for spring wildflowers, such as Virginia bluebells, sessile trillium, and Dutchman's breeches.

Since about 2000, I've seen or heard ravens around the McKee-Beshers Wildlife Management Area, farther down the Potomac than they had normally occurred. One day across the river from Sycamore Landing, a raven was harassing a bald eagle, and vice versa. Ravens are larger than crows, with a wedge-shaped tail and a hoarse "crruck" call.

Mile 27.5-29.3 – On the berm, beyond fringing trees, **Summit Hall Turf Farm** presents a large expanse of grass sometimes visited by migrating shorebirds in spring and late summer-early fall. Golden plovers and buff-breasted sandpipers have been seen in the latter season. Usually there are places where you can cross the canal bed for a look from the edge, but birders are no longer welcome on the turf farm itself because of past irresponsible behavior.

The American golden plover is magnificently plumaged in spring, with black underparts, gold-flecked back, and white on the side of the neck. When it returns from its Arctic breeding grounds it is losing this plumage and some have the gray winter plumage. They are then on their way to South America. Besides turf farms, they are often seen on plowed fields. The dainty little buff-breasted sandpiper is also on its way from the Arctic to South American wintering grounds. While feeding, it swings back and forth, picking invertebrates from the surface of the ground.

Mile 29 – Maryland DNR flights from 2002 to 2004 recorded an **eagle's nest** on Selden Island, across the river.

Mile 30.5 – Chisel Branch Hiker-Biker.

Mile 30.9 – Lock 25 and **Edwards Ferry**. Upstream from Edwards Ferry one might begin watching for **fox squirrels**, which are larger than gray squirrels, with orange-tinged belly and tail. They are most common above Harpers Ferry and seem to prefer the lowlands. Fox squirrels are most partial to open woods, the gray squirrel to denser woods. Canal travelers along the upper reaches may occasionally see the chipmunk-sized red squirrel, a feisty creature that likes woods with conifers and ranges north to treeline in Canada and Alaska.

Mile 31 – The forest on the river side of the canal was mostly wet, grassy **old fields** in the 1950s—a place where you might expect to see snipe. Now there are box elders and other trees up to one foot thick. Fence remnants along the towpath indicate this was once pasture. Such old fields have been a prominent part of the landscape along the canal since late in the nineteenth century, when competition with farmers in the Midwest and continuing difficulty of access across the canal to their land began discouraging farmers on the Maryland shore of the Potomac. The park service tries to maintain some of the historical landscape by arrangements with farmers, but this particular piece of land wasn't included. A very rough approximation of the age of trees on former old fields might be 50 years per foot of diameter, although tree size varies greatly with species and site characteristics.

Mile 32.6 – This power line crossing is dense with meadow-like vegetation in summer. An interesting change after miles of shadowy forest, this swath of tall grasses and composites should be attractive to butterflies.

About two miles of turf farms extend upstream from here. Screened by trees, they are difficult to see from the towpath. Determined birders may be able to find places to cross the canal bed to scan for shorebirds in season.

Paw Paw

In places the towpath is lined with paw paws, a small tree up to 20 or 30 feet high that flourishes in moist forest from New Jersey and southern Michigan to northern Florida and eastern Texas. It has large—up to a foot-long—oblong leaves. The dark purplish flowers bloom in April and May as the leaves are coming out. What is most notable about this tree is its large, pendant fruit, which in our area ripens from early September to mid-October. Aficionados seek it out for its soft, sweet flesh, which tastes rather like mango. They eat it raw, cooked, and in other ways, such as ice cream. (Collection of such fruits is allowed by the park service.) These fruits can be hard to find, because opossums, squirrels, raccoons, foxes, and other wild creatures like them too.

Paw paw flower photo by Connie Durnan.

Mile 34.3 – Turtle Run Hiker-Biker.

Mile 34.5 – Nests of **great blue herons** are visible in winter from the boat ramp at Whites Ferry on a small island just downstream. For a good view of the breeding activity in spring and summer you need to walk down the shore through the grounds of the private Whites Ferry Sportsman's Club. Request permission. The heron colony had about 30 nests in 2008. A great egret was seen carrying a stick toward this island during an earlier breeding season and may have nested here. If so, this was probably the farthest inland nesting of great egrets in Maryland. Most of their colonies in the state are around Chesapeake Bay and the Atlantic coast.

Mile 34.9 – Stretching from the upstream end of Harrison Island to the Maryland shore, a V-shaped arrangement of rocks, with the point downstream, is visible during low water. This is a fish trap, built to channel fish so they could be netted. Such traps, called fish pots by local people today, are common along the river; between Point of Rocks and Harpers Ferry alone, 36 have been identified. Though Indians may have used such traps, those remaining now are thought to have been built in colonial times or later.

Mile 35.5 – Whites Ferry.

Mile 38.2 – Marble Quarry Hiker-Biker.

Mile 38.6 – A bluff of red sandstone 30 to 100 feet high is festooned with ferns.

Mile 39.4 – Lock 26. A giant **silver maple** over six feet in diameter stands between the lock and flume. Silver maples usually don't grow as big as sycamores, but this one is an exception. (See Overview: Floodplain Trees for more about this common species.)

Mile 39.6 – Parking place for the **Dickerson Conservation Area**. Most of its 305 acres are on the berm side, which is a public hunting area, but there's also a strip on the river side. A trail leads to the river and then upstream to the outlet of the flume from the Dickerson Power Plant. The shoreline plume of warm water attracts fish and fishermen in winter, who say it is warm enough to wade in. Apparently the plant does not discharge warm effluent every day, however.

The river side of the canal is very good for wildflowers in spring and on scour bars in the river in summer.

The canal is watered from Mile 39.6 to Lock 27 (Mile 41.5). **Beavers** have built several lodges on the berm of the watered section. Fresh cuttings can be seen in the woods adjacent to the towpath. From here on, I will point out only the more interesting works of beavers. By now you probably know, if you didn't already, what their lodges, dams, and tree-cutting look like. These features are frequent along the canal, much of which can be considered active or disused beaver ponds.

Numerous dead trees in these woods help to attract **woodpeckers**. In winter six species can be seen: downy, hairy, red-bellied (the red on top of the head is more easily seen), the large, black and white pileated, flicker, and yellow-bellied sapsucker. The scarcer red-headed (a striking red, white, and blue, with the whole head red) is an additional, slight possibility. Most of the mature woods along the canal harbor the first six mentioned above, though the sapsuckers are farther north in summer.

Zebra Swallowtail

From late March to October, it's likely that these black-and-white striped butterflies with the long tails will flit across your path. Though it nectars on many kinds of flowers, the zebra swallowtail's eggs are laid only on paw paw leaves, which the larvae eat when they emerge. (See box on paw paw, page 33.) Thus the zebra swallowtail is largely restricted to lowland forests where most paw paws grow. Other swallowtails along the towpath include the common tiger and spicebush swallowtails, the less common black swallowtail, and the rather rare giant and pipevine swallowtails.

Photo by Connie Durnan.

Mile 40.6 – The **Dickerson Power Plant's** three smokestacks are visible from miles around. Environmentalists fought building of the plant in some of Montgomery County's prime agricultural land in the 1960s and addition of a garbage incinerator in 1990. They describe it as one of the dirtiest power plants in the county—just meeting the relaxed standards of 2005. The plant gets some good public relations, however, from its part in turning the effluent channel into an artificial slalom run, where kayakers practiced for the 1992 Summer Olympics and members of the U.S. Whitewater Slalom Team continue to practice.

Mile 41.5 – Lock 27.

Mile 41.9 – A culvert carries the **Little Monocacy River** under the canal. It rises on the east side of Sugarloaf Mountain, four miles away.

Aqueduct near the mouth of the Monocacy River, an area where Indians fished and grew crops.

Mile 42.2 – Constructed of pink quartzite from Sugarloaf Mountain and often damaged by floods, the **Monocacy Aqueduct** was repaired in 2005. The **Monocacy River**, largest of the Potomac tributaries on the Maryland side upstream from Washington, has been designated a State Scenic River. With headwaters in Pennsylvania and on Catoctin Mountain, it served Indians camped on river terraces at its mouth (from about 1000 BCE until 1600 CE) as a travel route. From Catoctin Mountain they brought down rhyolite, a glassy volcanic rock that was much in demand as a trade item among tribes of the central Atlantic seaboard.

Their campsites at the mouth offered good fishing and fertile cropland.

The Monocacy River makes a pleasant, undemanding canoe run. It is usually runnable from late fall to mid-July, from Harney Road near the Pennsylvania border to its mouth, and after good rains, from Route 77 on down in late summer and fall as well. Edward Gertler, in *Maryland and Delaware Canoe Trails*, calls the scenery "remarkably consistent, typified by a wooded bluff on one side, fields and farms on the other, and a million gawking cattle." The only hazard is a three-foot weir about two miles below Harney Road, which should be carried around. Bryan MacKay, in *Hiking, Cycling & Canoeing in Maryland*, says, "A canoe trip down the Monocacy will never be the most scenic, the most exciting, the most pristine, but the river will impress you, much like an old friend, with its quiet good nature." He recommends the 6.3 miles from Lilypons Road to Mouth of Monocacy as normally runnable any time of year.

Mile 42.4 – Indian Flats Hiker-Biker.

Mile 44 – Tuscarora Creek, which rises a few miles away on the southern part of Catoctin Mountain, passes under the canal through a culvert.

Mile 44.6 – Nolands Ferry. An eagle's nest near Nolands Ferry was reported to me without a precise location, the only one I know of on the Maryland shore above Washington. These eagles tolerate trains roaring past on the canal berm.

Mile 46.7-48.2 – Heaters Island is a Maryland wildlife management area. From 1699 until 1712, Coney-Piscataway Indians had a village here. Artifacts from the Woodland and Archaic periods have been found on several other large islands in the upper Potomac.

Mile 47.1 – A trail across the railroad tracks to Camp Kanawha, cabins owned by the Frederick County Fish and Game Protective Association, passes between two outcroppings of "**calico rocks**." This is a conglomerate of pebbles cemented in a matrix of gray-to-red limestone. This rock also outcrops across the river in Virginia. Along U.S. 15 north of Leesburg, near the side road to Whites Ferry, you can see its bumpy, elephantine shapes rising from the fields.

Mile 47.6 – Kanawha Spring, a pool 15-feet across, lies in a deep depression, enclosed by a fence, on the river side of the canal. The water comes through fissures in the limestone conglomerate and flows out to the Potomac.

Mile 47.7 – Calico Rocks Hiker-Biker, named for the rocks described above.

Mile 48.4 – A sign under the Route 15 bridge warns about the **northern snakehead**, an exotic Asian fish recently found in the Potomac below Washington. A voracious predator weighing up to 15 pounds, it reproduces prolifically and probably poses a threat to native fishes. Fishermen are told to kill any snakehead they catch and report it to the Maryland DNR. As of January 2006 none had been reported above Little Falls.

Mile 48.4-48.6 – Point of Rocks Tunnel. This railroad tunnel is cut through **greenstone** of the Catoctin Formation. Greenstone was originally a Precambrian lava that underwent metamorphism near the end of the Precambrian. A second tunnel through greenstone extends from Mile 49.8 to 50.3. You can also see this rock where I-70 crosses Catoctin Mountain, at the crest.

Ravens often nest on the cliffs at Point of Rocks. In North America, ravens occupy wild country from tundra to northern and western forests, deserts, and mountains. In the Appalachians, ravens usually nest on cliffs, though trees are occasionally used. Larger than crows, they have a wedge-shaped tail and a long, heavy bill. They don't say "nevermore" but do utter a deep, throaty "crruk," distinct from a crow's "caw." Sometimes they soar, like hawks, or perform acrobatic aerial displays. A truly intriguing bird.

Mile 49 – Lock 28. Bamboo planted beside the lockhouse has formed a dense stand. Though it has many uses in Asia, I suppose this tough exotic was planted here as an ornamental.

Mile 50.3 – Bald Eagle Island Hiker-Biker was presumably named for an island opposite this site where eagles once nested.

Mile 50.5 – Precambrian greenish-gray **schist** is exposed in an outcrop along the railroad.

Mile 50.6 – Poplar Branch passes under the canal.

Mile 50.9 – Lock 29.

Mile 51.4 – Blue to green-gray **gneiss** outcrops along the railroad. Gneiss is a metamorphic rock often formed from granite. It has a banded appearance.

Mile 51.5 – On a bridge over one remaining arch of an aqueduct, the towpath crosses **Catoctin Creek**, which drains the Middletown Valley, between Catoctin Mountain and South Mountain.

Mile 52.5 – Little Catoctin Creek passes under the canal.

Mile 54.2 – The **Brunswick Recreation Area**, run by the town, offers picnic and camping sites, boat rentals, and launching ramp.

Mile 54.5 – Brunswick Waste Water Treatment Plant.

Mile 55 – Lock 30.

Mile 55.1 – The **NPS Visitor Center** at Brunswick is accessible from the towpath through a large parking lot, past the train station on South Maple Street, and left one block on Potomac Street to the corner at Maryland Avenue. The entrance to the visitor center is through the adjacent Railroad Museum. The visitor center exhibits emphasize local history and the area's relation of the canal and railroad.

Mile 57 – Knoxville (or Paynes) **Branch** passes under the canal.

Mile 57.7 – Cliffs on South Mountain expose **Weverton quartzite**, a very hard Cambrian rock that forms this mountain ridge. The quartzite began as sandy sediments, probably laid down by rivers or on beaches.

Mile 58 – Lock 31. The **Appalachian Trail**, marked by vertical white blazes, comes down from South Mountain onto the towpath, which it follows to the railroad bridge across the Potomac at Mile 60.7. The trail runs over 2100 miles from Springer Mountain in Georgia to Mount Katahdin in Maine. The Appalachian Trail Conference headquarters is in Harpers Ferry at the intersection of Washington and Jackson streets. (See Side Trip: The Appalachian Trail on South Mountain.)

Water Quality in the Potomac

Potomac River water quality has had its ups and downs. From the early 1900s to the 1960s it got progressively worse. In 1965 President Lyndon Johnson called the Potomac "a national disgrace." Federal clean water laws of the late 1960s and early 1970s facilitated a turnaround, establishing monitoring and other state requirements. Billions of dollars nationwide were pumped into the cleanup effort. A one billion dollar investment in municipal waste water treatment plants in the Potomac basin between the mid-1960s and the mid-'80s received much of the credit for the remarkable improvement that occurred. "Compared to the late '60s and early '70s," an environmental planner with the Metropolitan Washington Council of Governments said, "the Potomac is a whole new river." Fish and plant life had made a strong comeback, and some parts of the river had been once again declared swimmable. However, further progress since the 1980s has been slow. Loads of sediment, nitrogen, and phosphorous have been reduced, mainly because of the loss of farmland, but loss of forests, and pollutant-laden runoff from rapid urban development counter that trend. The Potomac Conservancy says, "the health of the river has reached a plateau," and awards it a D+. Presumably, this contrasts with an F in the 1960s. For further details see The Potomac Conservancy website: www.potomac.org

Mile 58.2 – Israel Creek, which drains the narrow valley between South Mountain and the Blue Ridge, tumbles over rocks and passes under the canal through a large culvert.

Mile 58.7 – There's a large nest, probably of eagles, on an island across the river. Some 20 great blue heron nests can be seen in the leafless season about a quarter-mile upstream on this island.

Mile 59.3-60.7 – Geologists do not agree about the age and history of the **Potomac River.** However it originated, the river eroded as fast as the earth rose, maintaining its path across the grain of the rocks. From below the U.S. 340 bridge to the railroad bridge to Harpers Ferry, you can see during low water the layers of rocks through which the river had to cut. Appearing as ledges and scattered islands, these layers can be recognized by their colors. Below and for about 1,000 feet upstream from the 340 bridge are islands of light-colored gneiss, a very old "basement" rock. Then you pass about 1,000 feet of greenstone. Next comes 3,100 feet of white Weverton quartzite, the principal rock of the Blue Ridge. Beyond the railroad bridge is dark Harpers phyllite, shale that also has been transformed by powerful earth pressures. All these bands of rock continue in the ridges on either side of the river. The Blue Ridge is an anticline—an upfold in the earth—that has been overturned toward the west, or upstream. Therefore the gneiss is the bottom, oldest layer, and the phyllite, the youngest of the series, represents the top of the fold. The river in its cutting has revealed the earliest earth products in the Potomac region.

Mile 60.2 – Lock 32.

The quartzite and metagraywacke rocks of Maryland Heights were once a nesting place for peregrines, which chose a sheltered ledge on the cliff. *Photo by Connie Durnan.*

Mile 60.7 – Lock 33. The railroad emerges from a tunnel through the Weverton quartzite and metagraywacke of Maryland Heights and crosses the river.

The mountain cliffs around Harpers Ferry attract black vultures, turkey vultures, and ravens. **Peregrine falcons** once nested on the high cliff at Maryland Heights but succumbed, with other peregrines nesting in the Appalachians, to effects of long-lasting pesticides, which caused eggshell thinning. Happily, recovery of the peregrine is underway. At many sites in the eastern U.S. and elsewhere, young birds have been raised in "hack boxes," fed by people they can't see to avoid imprinting on humans. After several years of this, they sometimes return to the area as adults and breed. This is the hope at Maryland Heights, where hacking of peregrines was conducted from 2001 to 2005.

Hemmed in as it is between rocky walls, with little or no flood plain on which to spread excess water, the Potomac at Harpers Ferry has always been hard on the canal during high water. The lockhouses in this stretch have been torn to their foundations by **floods**, and the towpath has been breached repeatedly. Several road and railroad bridges have met a similar fate.

Mile 61.5 – Lock 34.

Mile 61.7-62 – On the berm are good exposures of **phyllite** of the Harpers Formation.

Across the river, Harpers Ferry sits on this same metamorphic rock type. Phyllite is slate that has undergone further heat and pressure and has a silky sheen on freshly broken surfaces. (Farther back in time, metamorphism produced the slate from shale, a fine-grained sedimentary rock composed of silt- and clay-sized particles.)

Mile 62.3 – Lock 35.

Mile 62.5 – Lock 36.

Mile 62.9 – Huckleberry Hill Hiker-Biker.

Side Trip: Rock Creek Park

The walker going up Rock Creek from the canal follows first the busy Rock Creek Parkway and then, past the National Zoo, enters Rock Creek Park, which widens and extends to the Maryland line—1,754 acres of mostly forested hills managed by the National Park Service. It is a natural green oasis flanked by city. If he or she wants to, the walker can follow the creek north into Maryland, through 4,500 more acres of parkland.

Rock Creek drops 165 feet from the Maryland line to tidewater at the Potomac, gliding and tumbling from the Piedmont through the Fall Zone to the Coastal Plain. It first traverses recent alluvium deposited since the last ice age, through a broad flood plain, then moves more swiftly over boulders of gneiss and schist through a narrow valley, and then quietly empties into the river.

The park offers 30 miles of trails, some of which are open to bikers and horseback riders. For the first couple of miles, along the parkway, one faces a flood of commuters in cars and on bicycles. Despite all the noise and motion, you might spot a kingfisher, wood duck, or hawk.

Great blue heron near the Pierce Mill Dam.

Welcome tranquility begins where the road goes through a tunnel while the trail loops around, following the creek. Here you are apt to see mallards poking around the shoreline waters, and other species, not expected in an urban park, such as great blue herons, red-tailed and red-shouldered hawks, and pileated woodpeckers, might show up. Off to the west, across the creek, you could see a hulking bear ambling around at the foot of a cliff. This is a sloth bear, a tropical species in the National Zoo, where animals are kept in semi-natural surroundings.

Perhaps the presence of zoo animals in a wooded environment attracts wild animals. This was certainly the case when wild black-crowned night herons began nesting in a tree outside a cage containing their confreres, years ago. They still nest around the bird house, flying off in the evening to hunt, sometimes along Rock Creek, more often along the Potomac. Vultures used to roost at the Kennedy Warren, an apartment house next to the zoo, prompting the joke that they were probably waiting for the old folks living there to die.

Deer are now regulars in the park. Though occasionally showing up in ones and twos over the years, they weren't common in Rock Creek Park until the late 1980s, when a small herd apparently moved in to stay and reproduce. A night-time infrared aerial survey in March 1997 recorded 86 deer, and that same year 30 were killed by cars in the park. More recent surveys have been conducted from roads by spot-lighting; the estimate in fall 2005 was 200 deer. A similar survey in November 2008 gave an estimate of 55 deer per square mile and a total of 220 deer in the four-square-mile park. Monitored vegetation plots have shown a major impact of deer feeding on plants. Residents at the edge of the park complain about deer eating *their* plants.

Aside from deer, gray squirrels, and chipmunks, mammals are not often seen in Rock Creek, but many are there: red and gray foxes, opossums, southern flying squirrels, small rodents, raccoons, and others. Raccoons are quite common and apparently wander widely. One radio-collared raccoon traveled from far up in the park, across Memorial Bridge into Virginia, and back into the park. Muskrats and three or four families of beavers inhabit the creek. The beavers use bank dens. Rock Creek is too swift and flood-prone for beaver dams and lodges.

Above Pierce Mill at Park Road you have two main trail choices for walking: the Valley Trail along Rock Creek, and the Western Ridge Trail on the hills west of the creek. Along the Valley Trail you can enjoy the stream's pools and riffles and watch for kingfishers and wood ducks. The Western Ridge Trail takes you through a quiet forest, remote from car noise on Beach Drive.

Both trails wind through forests of oaks, tulip trees, beech, and other species with trees up to 100 years old. Although a few large oaks over 275 years old have been found, no old growth stands remain. Before establishment of the park in 1890, farms and orchards occupied much of the land, and timber cutting took other trees. During the Civil War, a band of forest 1 1/2 miles wide was cleared north of Military Road so guns at forts DeRussey and Stevens would have an open field of fire. After park establishment, many sun-loving pines entered the regrowing forest, but today only scattered Virginia pines are noticeable among the canopy trees. Altogether, more than 650 species of vascular plants have been recorded in the park, but because of the land's history and the adjacent urban areas, more than one-third of these species are exotics (introduced non-natives).

In winter the leafless trees display their basic architecture: the smooth gray trunks of beech, the straighter shafts of fast-growing tulip trees, and the muscular branches of white, black, and chestnut oaks. That time of year most of the woodland birds are in flocks. You go for some time without a bird, then you are in the midst of chickadees, titmice, white-breasted nuthatches, Carolina wrens, and woodpeckers. Watch, too, for the diminutive winter wren, which likes log piles and stream banks. Its sharp "jip jip" call may alert you to its presence.

Christmas Bird Counts (part of a hemisphere-wide program sponsored by the National Audubon Society) give a broader picture of the park's winter bird life. A large section of Rock Creek Park is covered each year as part of the Washington, D.C. count. During the 1990s these counts yielded great horned, barred, and screech owls; red-tailed, red-shouldered, and sharp-shinned hawks and American kestrels; and uncommon woodland birds such as brown creepers, golden-crowned kinglets, and hermit thrushes. Mallards and wood ducks, the latter scarce in winter around Washington, are regulars.

Birders spot numerous migrants at this forest opening south of the Rock Creek Nature Center.

In the spring, Rock Creek's green band through the city attracts migrating birds looking for a place to put down and feed. Early in the morning, the Western Ridge Trail, between Broad Branch Road and Military Road, is an especially favored area. Perhaps best of all is an opening in the forest about 1/2 mile south of the Nature Center, just beyond the park maintenance yard. Migrants begin congregating here when the sun first hits the treetops. These flocks contain birds returning from the southern U.S. and farther south, such as vireos, flycatchers, thrushes, and many warblers. Southbound birds in fall also favor these spots.

For several years Wallace Kornack, a retired mechanical engineer, has kept meticulous daily records of spring and fall migrants in this part of Rock Creek

Park, in both fair weather and rain. His lists show great diversity and interesting chronological trends. He can be contacted at Wallace@kornack.com.

Some of the migrating species stop to breed in the park, but the neotropical migrants among them have declined alarmingly in recent decades, as tropical forests are cleared and forests in North America are fragmented. A breeding bird census conducted on a 65-acre plot in Rock Creek Park almost annually since 1948 shows this trend. In 1997, six of the neotropical migrants recorded on the plot in 1948—yellow-throated vireo, hooded warbler, ruby-throated hummingbird, yellow-billed cuckoo, parula warbler, and Kentucky warbler—were not found. Others, like wood thrush, red-eyed vireo, and ovenbird (which, with the tufted titmouse, were still the most common breeders in the census area), were much reduced. The 2002 census showed the same losses.

In spite of all the polluted urban run-off captured by Rock Creek, the stream continues to support a surprising diversity of fish life. Among the nearly 40 species are smallmouth bass, largemouth bass, channel catfish, and bluegills, which people can fish for under D.C. regulations. But signs along the creek warn about eating them: "Fish from these waters contain PCBs and other chemical contaminants. Do not eat catfish, carp, or eel from these waters. You may eat 1/2 pound per month of largemouth bass or 1/2 pound per week of sunfish or other fish…."

Entrance to a fish ladder (at right side of Pierce Mill Dam). It gives migrating fish access to miles of spawning areas upstream.

In spring the age-old runs of alewives and blue-backed herring still occur, the alewives from mid-March to late April, and the blue-backs from late April to late May. Stream barriers in the lower section of Rock Creek have been removed and a fish ladder constructed at the Pierce Mill dam, so the fish can now travel past the D.C. line and perhaps farther. Eels, which carry out a reverse migration downstream to spawn in the Sargasso Sea, also benefit from the recent stream improvements.

Bob Ford, who watched over the park as its chief natural resource manager from 1976 to 2004, keenly understood the difficulty of maintaining a natural area in the midst of a city. "We're in an urban watershed," he said, "and all kinds of stuff are washed down – bacteria, other pollutants, sediments from construction." Resolution of this problem lay outside his hands. But his National Park Service associates *can* do something about another big problem – aggressive exotic plants like porcelainberry, Asiatic bittersweet, and Japanese honeysuckle, which climb and smother trees, and lesser celandine, which spreads in mats over the forest floor, displacing native spring plants. Kudzu, another exotic vine, has been almost eradicated, and the four species above perhaps could be as well, with sufficient funding.

Such threats, however, do not diminish the pleasure of walking in Rock Creek Park. One could still agree with the naturalist John Burroughs, writing in 1871:

> Rock Creek has an abundance of all the elements that make up not only pleasing but wild and rugged scenery. There is, perhaps, not another city in the Union that has on its very threshold so much natural beauty and grandeur, such as men seek for in remote forests and mountains.

Side Trip: Glover-Archbold Park

At Mile 1.5 on the towpath, a side trail leads through a large tunnel under the canal and north 3 miles through Glover-Archbold Park, also managed by the National Park Service. The trail crosses Reservoir Road, New Mexico Avenue, Cathedral Avenue, and Massachusetts Avenue, and ends at Van Ness Street. Tributary trails connect with Rock Creek Park to the east and Battery Kemble Park to the west.

The mature forest in Glover-Archbold Park displays all sizes of trees and many fallen giants.

This stream-valley park along Foundry Branch is in many ways a smaller version of Rock Creek Park. Its trees, predominantly oaks, hickories, tulip trees, and beech, are mostly the same, except that all, or nearly all, Virginia pines formerly present have died out with closure of the canopy, high overhead. One of the chief pleasures of a walk here is contemplating the majesty of mature forests. A couple of tulip trees near Reservoir Road have attained diameters of near four feet. Many giants have fallen, returning their nutrients to the soil. Part of the central section, on the west side, has a nearly pure stand of middle-aged tulip trees on a former farm field. Rather startling is a huge clump of introduced bamboo near the disused streetcar bridge at the south end of the park.

Small floodplains flank parts of the stream, but most of the terrain is hilly. Foundry Branch, however, being smaller and intermittent in summer, supports much less aquatic life than does Rock Creek. Wood ducks and mallards have nested along the stream, but don't look for fish, muskrats, or beavers.

Although residential neighborhoods press on both sides of this rather narrow park, Glover-Archbold remains a pleasantly green oasis with considerable variety of plants and animals. About two dozen deer reside here and make nightly forays into adjacent yards and gardens, hiding out during the day in thickets. You will probably see gray squirrels, maybe chipmunks, and possibly a red fox. Gray foxes, raccoons, and opossums, along with small rodents, are more active at night. For some years, barred and screech owls have been present. Red-shouldered hawks still nest here. With all the old or dead trees, woodpeckers flourish. You can see five species here in summer, including the big, showy pileated, and in winter six, when yellow-bellied sapsuckers move down from farther north. On an evening in early summer, listen to the ethereal chorus of veeries, a thrush that appeared as a breeder in the Washington area in the 1940s and now outnumbers the wood thrush in Glover-Archbold.

Beginning in 1959, the Audubon Naturalist Society conducted breeding bird censuses in the central part of Glover-Archbold Park. Shirley Briggs, leader of this project, was one of the first to report a decline of tropical migrants nesting in North America, as evidenced in these studies (and in those in Rock Creek Park and on Cabin John Island, in the Potomac). For instance, during the breeding bird census in 2005, no Kentucky or hooded warblers were found—both species regularly seen here in summer in the mid-twentieth century. However, Glover-Archbold, like Rock Creek Park, does attract migrants passing over the city, and sometimes the unexpected. One April I found a long-eared owl hiding in honeysuckle, and another spring an exploring yellow-crowned night heron.

Though it is set in the city and well-populated with joggers and dog-walkers, you can never rule out natural surprises in Glover-Archbold Park.

Side Trip: Great Falls and the Potomac Gorge

The Great Falls-Widewater area is a dramatic exhibit of geologic processes and the relation of plant cover to geology and flooding. Three very different sorts of environments have resulted: the rocky islands from Great Falls downstream (scoured bedrock terrace), flood plain forest above Great Falls, and wooded hills across the canal.

One warm June day Bob Johnsson, a former National Park Service interpreter who was an avid botanist, described to me the range of conditions plants must deal with on the islands:

> During floods the water pours through the rocky channels with great force. The lowest levels may be flooded several times a year. The surface of the higher islands is swept by floods on the average only every 20 years or so, as in 1972 and

1996. Between floods, which is most of the time, plants must be able to survive hot, dry conditions. The surface of the rocks can reach 140 degrees. Or, plants take advantage of small pools and damp areas where water collects and stays longer. So you get a mosaic of microhabitats that support the greatest diversity of plants anywhere in Maryland. Fifty or sixty species are found nowhere else in the state. Many of these exist here because they can tolerate drought and flooding and don't have to compete with common plants of the region that can't tolerate these conditions.

A low-level site is the Cropley scour bar, near Angler's Inn. Here rocky peninsulas that are often flooded project into the river. Bob pointed out many seedling sycamores that had sprung from crevices, as did flowering riverbank goldenrod, common on the rocks at all levels in the Mather Gorge area but not elsewhere in Maryland. Climbing dogbane, a vine of the southern coastal plain, was creeping over the rocks, and near a pool was the grass floating paspalum, whose only known Maryland/Virginia sites are here around Great Falls and along the river in Frederick County, Maryland.

One of the most interesting riverside plants in the rocky terrain below Great Falls is prairie redroot, a small shrub with showy white flowers. It was first discovered by a Smithsonian botanist on the flats in the Potomac gorge. Surprisingly, its principal range was later found to be the upper Midwest, with smaller, scattered populations in Quebec, Vermont, West Virginia, and other places to the west.

Perennials like prairie redroot are in the minority in the frequently flooded and occasionally ice-scoured zone below Great Falls. Such plants as mistflower, halberd-leaved rose mallow, and buttonweed survive by having deep root systems that can withstand the force of the water and send up new shoots when the water recedes. More common are annuals like ivy-leaved morning glory and carpet weed. Such plants can grow, flower, and fruit between floods, and their seeds can survive 10 to 15 years, giving them a long time in which to be washed or blown into a favorable germination site.

At mid-level sites, which have an intermediate flood frequency, Bob explained, trees like green ash, sassafras, and persimmon have time to grow taller and older, though often "beaten up." Grasses dominate many of the more open places. Patches of "prairie relicts" appear, so called because of the prevalence of prairie grasses like big and little bluestem and Indiangrass.

A grassy glade on Olmsted Island.

A boardwalk with bridges built to withstand floods leads out to Olmsted Island and a view of Great Falls. Atop Olmsted Island and its bedrock terrace, where only the highest floods reach, a forest of small to medium-sized Virginia pines, red, chestnut, and post oaks, green ash, red cedars, and other trees has become established. Among the rocks, the plants are mostly perennials, such as the common moss phlox and wild oat. Some of the rare plants in this zone are Canada milkvetch, narrow melic grass, wild false indigo, and hairy wild petunia—all endangered in Maryland.

Yet another environment is found on Sherwin Island, below Mather Gorge: wooded sand and gravel bars. Some of the common flood plain plants grow here, such as golden ragwort and yellow trout lily. But many rare plants, more common in other parts of the country, have been found, such as ostrich fern and star-flowered false Solomon's-seal (northern); rock skullcap (northern Appalachian); white trout lily, harbinger of spring, and Coville's phacelia (midwestern); and yellow passionflower, Virginia dayflower, and bloodleaf (southern).

The rare flora at Great Falls and the Potomac Gorge consists predominantly of midwestern species, with southern plants next most numerous, and northern least numerous. One can easily imagine that northern and southern species arrived here via the river and its valley, but how account for the midwestern ones? One theory is that they came during the dry hypsithermal period

5,000-6,000 years ago, when prairie extended into Ohio and possibly in patches into Pennsylvania. Like most of the other disjunct species in this area, they survive here partly because of reduced competition from the common plants of Maryland.

The flood plain forest upstream from the dam above Great Falls is much like the other flood plain forests upriver. Flood waters here are broad and slow. They knock down few trees and deposit silt. Large silver maples and sycamores, along with smaller boxelders, dominate this lush forest; paw paw and spicebush form dense undergrowth. In spring, masses of Virginia bluebells and golden ragwort carpet the ground, in company with less conspicuous violets, spring beauties, and other wildflowers. Shumard oak, a southern tree, is one of the few rare species found here, as it is in scattered other locations upriver and downriver. This is the habitat beloved by barred owls, and one can often be found not far up the towpath from Great Falls Tavern.

Wild false indigo, a rare plant in Maryland, grows atop Olmsted Island, out of reach of most floods. *Photo by Robert Johnsson, courtesy of Fanny Johnsson.*

Trails through the Gold Mine Tract across the canal offer walks through upland forest, distinctly different from the lowland forests that shade walkers and bikers along most of the towpath. In this upland, oaks and hickories rule, with tulip trees, beeches, and sugar maples mixed in. Dogwood, serviceberry, and black haw form much of the understory. As in eastern forests generally, early spring is the peak time for wildflowers, before the tree leaves are fully out and block the sunlight. Look especially in rich ravines for Dutchman's breeches, twinleaf, squirrel corn, bloodroot, wild ginger, ramps, sessile trillium, toothworts, violets, and spring beauties. Unfortunately, however, the wildflower display is not what it once was, because of grazing by the abundant deer. A distinct browse line has been created by their feeding on woody plants. (The flood plain forest, too, has suffered.) People love to see deer, but too many can lead to damage. No simple remedy is in sight. (See Overview: Managing the Park.) Canada geese have also proliferated and become tame around Great Falls Tavern, to the point of grazing the lawn bare and making a nuisance of themselves (see Milepost 14.4).

The Gold Mine Tract is named for a former mine (the Maryland Mine), now fenced and visible from MacArthur Boulevard. Gold, which occurred in small quantities within thick veins of quartz, was mined between 1867 and 1941.

Besides deer, beavers and wild turkeys are often seen around Great Falls. Once made rare by hunting and trapping, these animals have thrived under enlightened wildlife management. The prohibition against hunting and trapping in all of the C & O Canal National Historical Park has made these lands especially productive for such animals. An animal even more indicative of wildness has been seen here. One day a park policeman spotted a bobcat on the shore of the river downstream. Such things make Great Falls, so near metropolitan Washington, seem miles away.

Side Trip: McKee-Beshers Wildlife Management Area

About a mile north of the aqueduct over Seneca Creek, the red sandstone cliffs turn inland and describe a shallow arc that returns to the canal six miles upstream. Seneca Creek State Park parallels the canal for the first part of this lowland stretch and then, for four miles, comes the McKee-Beshers Wildlife Management Area.

McKee-Beshers, known to local birders as Hughes Hollow, is a 2,000-acre mosaic of swampy woods, fields, hedgerows, and diked ponds. These features lie in what may have been a former channel of the Potomac. The water flow is now regulated by the Maryland Department of Natural Resources, creating seasonally flooded "green-tree reservoirs" and varying levels in the open ponds. The DNR plants sorghum, millet, and sunflowers for wildlife; farmers plant corn and soybeans, for wildlife and themselves. The whole area is laced with tracks and trails, giving good access to hunters, nature enthusiasts, and just plain walkers.

Hunters pursue deer, turkeys, ducks, doves, rabbits, and squirrels here. Other people should be aware of hunting seasons and wear orange at those times. Hunting begins with mourning doves September 1. Deer bow, gun, and muzzle-loader seasons run at various times between mid-September and January 31; squirrel hunting October to January; rabbits November to early February; and turkeys mid-April to mid-May. Deer firearm season—the last week of November and first week of December—might be a good time for non-hunters to avoid, except on Sunday, when hunting is not permitted. Check with the Maryland DNR for hunting regulations and open seasons.

Dog training is conducted in various fields and pen-reared quail, chukars (a Eurasian partridge introduced to the western U.S.), and sometimes pheasants are released then. Apparently, none of these birds survive to reproduce, least of all the chukars, who are totally out of their normal dry, rocky hill habitat.

Diked ponds at McKee-Beshers Wildlife Management Area attract many waterbirds as well as the electric blue-backed tree swallow. *Swallow photo by Connie Durnan.*

McKee-Beshers, with such a variety of habitats plus the adjacent Potomac River, is one of the best birding areas near Washington. Paul Woodward, a local birder, has recorded over 230 species here. Unexpected vagrants, such as the purple gallinule and swallow-tailed kite, have appeared. Typical birds of the swamp forests are wood ducks, red-shouldered hawks, and barred owls. Woodpeckers abound. This is one of the best places around Washington to see the scarce red-headed. Good places to look for it are along Horsepen Branch, near its crossing of Sycamore Landing Road, and just west of the diked ponds. At these ponds look for willow flycatchers and tree swallows, which nest in boxes placed here for them. The tree swallows arrive in March, and migrating ducks, such as ring-necked ducks, sometimes assemble here in early spring. Among my more unusual sightings at the ponds were a red-throated loon, and a sora rail standing on a willow branch during high water. At dusk one May evening I watched a yellow-crowned night heron flying over; these herons, a southern bird, have nested at McKee-Beshers for many years, but they're rather hard to find. Since at least 2009 great egrets have been at the ponds area and may nest. The dense stand of Norway spruce just west of the ponds has sheltered wintering owls, such as saw-whet. In March try the fields at the canal end of Sycamore Landing Road around dusk for woodcocks performing their courtship flights.

Participants in the Seneca Christmas Bird Count always search Hughes Hollow carefully. In summer, the western Montgomery County butterfly count does likewise, because butterfly diversity here parallels that of birds. Dick Smith and Philip Kean have recorded at least 81 species in this area.

In late summer many flowers are in bloom in the fields and ponds at Hughes Hollow. Among the species around the ponds are the swamp rose mallow, halberd-leaved rose mallow, and purple fringeless orchid.

Our Native American predecessors also appreciated the fertile soils and abundant wildlife of Hughes Hollow. Prehistoric occupation goes back to Paleo-Indians, some 12,000 years ago, but evidence of the most recent Woodland groups is much more abundant. One such site, occupied about 600 years ago, lies about 250 yards from the river. Excavated during the 1990s by archeologists from American University, the Hughes site revealed a stockaded village of perhaps 150 to 250 people who lived here for 50 to 75 years, then moved on. They raised corn, beans, and squash, hunted deer, elk, bear, mountain lion, raccoon, birds, and turtles. They used crushed shells of river mussels to temper the clay of their pottery. So rich in resources was this area that 99 other archeological sites have been found within two miles of the Hughes site—52 in Maryland and 47 in Virginia. (See Overview: Indian Life in the Valley.)

Campers along the canal who want to investigate the McKee-Beshers Wildlife Management Area can pitch their tents at the Horsepen Branch Hiker-Biker, at Mile 26. Day visitors can reach it from Washington by following River Road and then left on Route 112 (still River Road) for 4.5 miles. A left turn on Hughes Road will take you to the ponds. The next left off of River Road, onto Sycamore Landing Road, leads to a parking area at the canal.

Side Trip: The Appalachian Trail on South Mountain

The blooms of mountain laurel in late May and June brighten a walk on South Mountain. *Photos by Connie Durnan.*

A walk along the Appalachian Trail on South Mountain provides a pleasant contrast with the river valley scenes along the canal. Here you can look out occasionally upon the farmland below and see in the continuous forest on the ridge a somewhat different assortment of plants and animals. Spring and fall are probably the best times to hike the trail. Spring gives you the blooming of pink lady's-slipper and the shrub pinxter-flower (May) and mountain laurel (late May-June); also migrating birds such as warblers, vireos, and thrushes, especially in May. Fall offers tree color and migrating raptors. But any season is enjoyable.

The Maryland section of the Appalachian Trail is 40 miles long, running from the Potomac River at Harpers Ferry to the Pennsylvania line. Most sections are easy walking, with gradual slopes. The Potomac Appalachian Trail Club has done a good job of maintaining the trail and marking it with white blazes. They've even put stepping stones on some of the steeper places. Blue blazes mark side trails to shelters, overlooks, and other points of interest. Newcomers to backpacking might well start here. Shelters and other camping places are located at conveniently short intervals. Most of the Appalachian Trail in Maryland runs through South Mountain State Park, which provides a forested buffer. Some private property lies near the trail and must be respected.

The wildlife entertainment as you walk along will be mostly birds, varied occasionally by squirrels and chipmunks, sometimes a deer; but it's fun to know that such shy, seldom-seen animals as bobcats, and even bears, are in the woods with you. South Mountain now has a permanent population of black bears, mainly north of I-70. In season, tiger swallowtails, mourning cloaks, and other butterflies enliven the scene.

Though heavily forested now, South Mountain was cut over for charcoal from the eighteenth to the early twentieth century, and then for lumber. Farms occupied some of the gaps and lower slopes. In places you can discern some of this history. At Turners Gap, for instance, piles of stones and abundant tall, slender, tulip trees proclaim former fields or pastures. The disastrous loss of chestnuts early in the twentieth century was not total. A few smooth gray stumps remain, preserved this long by their tannin. Nearby may be seen chestnut sprouts, which grow until the fungus that killed the parent trees gets them too.

The forest has recovered nicely from logging; some of the trees are nearly 3 feet in diameter, a substantial size. I once counted annual rings in a foot and a half thick red oak that had fallen across the trail and been cut. There were about 60 rings, close together at first, indicating slow growth, and then farther apart as the tree got more sunlight.

During that walk, I composed a casual inventory of tree and shrub species seen. Most common were red oak, chestnut oak, red maple, the smaller sassafras, paw paw (strange to see paw paws up on the ridge), and mountain laurel. There were middling numbers of white oak, tulip tree, hickories, black gum, black birch, beech, and the smaller witch hazel, maple-leaved viburnum, sprouting chestnuts, and spicebush. I saw just one or a few ash, sugar maple, butternut, black cherry, Virginia pine, white pine, slippery elm, basswood, serviceberry, and black locust.

Later, farther north, I encountered scattered hemlocks. So, though the tree cover of South Mountain, like that of much of the eastern mountains, is categorized as Appalachian oak forest, there is nevertheless considerable variety.

On the east side of the ridge you often see gray rocks through the trees. These are outcroppings of the quartzite that tops most of the ridge. The rocks, with their many deep crevices, look like good denning areas for foxes and bobcats, as well as copperheads and timber rattlesnakes (which, however, you are not likely to see unless you go hunting for them).

The birds in mid-summer are rather quiet, but in addition to the permanent residents such as chickadees, titmice, white-breasted nuthatches, and woodpeckers, you are likely to see nesting tropical migrants: yellow-billed cuckoos, wood pewees, wood thrushes, scarlet tanagers, red-eyed vireos, ovenbirds, and perhaps a worm-eating warbler. Gray squirrels, red squirrels, chipmunks, white-tailed deer, and garter snakes are other common vertebrates.

Among the less reliable denizens are ruffed grouse and wild turkeys, which also breed on South Mountain. You may hear the croak of a raven as it travels the ridge. Some birds of northerly range, which you wouldn't see in summer along nearby parts of the canal, have been recorded on South Mountain; among them are black-capped chickadee, blue-headed vireo, blue-winged and chestnut-sided warbler, and rose-breasted grosbeak.

The view from Weverton Cliff is one of the best on the entire Appalachian Trail.
Photo by Connie Durnan.

Fall highlights, as mentioned, are tree color and migrating raptors. For best foliage displays, try mid- to late October. Several rock outcrops provide outstanding views. The Weverton cliffs near the Potomac give a splendid look at the river rapids below and the mountain ridges to the south.

For raptor watching, one well-known place is Washington Monument, near Turner's Gap and Alternate Route 40. From the top of this cream-bottle-shaped monument to George Washington one gets a good view north and west, but trees partially obscure the east view. Only about six or eight people can comfortably occupy the top at one time, so if you come here for hawk-watching, week days might be best.

The view north from High Rock, the direction from which migrating hawks come in the fall. *Photo by Connie Durnan.*

High Rock, two miles from the Pennsylvania line, was a favorite launching site for hang-gliders, but hang-gliding is no longer permitted here because of several deaths. You can drive to it from Penn-Mar or walk to it along the Appalachian Trail from Penn-Mar or an equal distance going north from Raven Rock Road. On the west side of the ridge, High Rock provides an excellent view west and north, which are the directions hawk-watchers need to look when there's a westerly wind. When there's a south or east wind, raptors tend to fly along the east side of the ridge.

Annapolis Rock, 2.2 miles north from I-70, is favored by rock-climbers. The west view here is good, but the north view extends only to a nearby side ridge. My favorite lookout spot is Black Rock, one mile farther north. There are good views here to the south, west, and north.

For best fall raptor-watching at sites such as these, one should know a bit about dates and weather conditions. The best conditions occur a day or two after a major cold front has passed through, with north or northwest winds.

The fall migration begins in August, with peaks in September for broad-wings, bald eagles, ospreys, and American kestrels. Late September is the best time for peregrines. Highest numbers of sharp-shinned and Cooper's hawks and merlins are reached in October. The beginning of November is considered the best time to look for red-tails, red-shoulders, northern harriers, turkey vultures, northern goshawks, golden eagles, and rough-legged hawks. Spring raptor migrations in the Appalachians usually have fewer birds. The peak then is late April and early May, on westerly winds.

This sport, though at times exciting, takes patience. You may have long periods when nothing goes by. That is a good time to haul out the coffee thermos or reminisce with your birding buddies about big hawk days of the past.

Travelers on the Maryland AT should be aware that the trail passes through two hunting areas in South Mountain State Park. One lies between Gathland State Park and Lambs Knoll, the other between I-70 and Wolfsville Road (which happens to be the most popular section for hikers). Since the Appalachian Trail corridor is generally only 500 feet wide on either side and its boundaries may not be marked, approaching hunters may not realize they are on AT land. Especially in deer firearm season—late November to early December—it's a good idea to wear blaze orange.

For detailed information on the trail in Maryland, see the *Appalachian Trail Guide to Maryland and Northern Virginia* and companion maps, published by the Potomac Appalachian Trail Club and available at local outdoor stores.

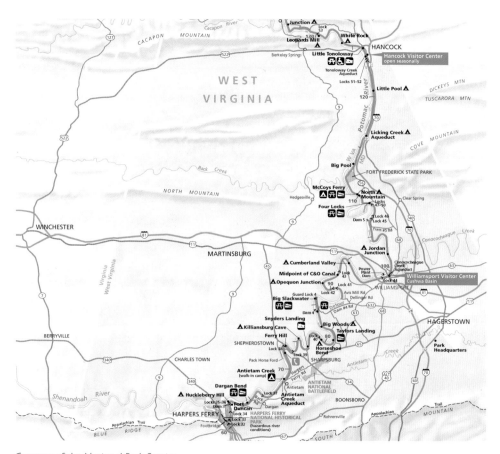

Courtesy of the National Park Service.

Harpers Ferry to Hancock

This section traverses the wide Great Valley, with its limestone and dolomite bedrock, which outcrops along the canal in many bluffs. The calcareous soil supports a rich diversity of plant life, some of it quite rare. Upstream from Fort Frederick State Park one gets into sandstone country, which forms low mountains to the north and south, but these are not easily seen from the towpath, sunk in its valley.

Mile 63-63.3 – Tomstown dolomite outcrops on the berm, a foretaste of much more to come upstream. Just beyond is an outcrop of **Antietam sandstone**, a resistant rock that forms some of the ridges in Maryland, though it is not as resistant as Weverton quartzite, which forms the highest ridges. The Antietam, Harpers, and Weverton formations, through which you have just passed, are all Cambrian in age, about 500 million years old.

Mile 65.2 – The brick-lined **Shinhan kilns** on the berm, which operated until the 1960s, are situated in Tomstown dolomite, which differs from limestone by the presence of magnesium. The rock was burned probably for plaster or fertilizer. Just upstream is the old quarry. Outcrops of Tomstown dolomite occur here and there up to about Mile 68.5.

Mile 66.5 – North-facing dolomite bluffs and bottomland along the canal provide cool, moist habitat for a **rich diversity of plant life**. In late March harbinger-of-spring blooms in the bottomlands and in April twinleaf, wild ginger, blue cohosh, and others. The rock outcrops are covered with wild columbine, several species of rock cress, early saxifrage, alumroot, miterwort, wild stonecrop, and green violet. High up one can find hispid buttercup, heart-leaved Alexanders, wild blue phlox, round-leaved ragwort, and shooting star.

Such north-facing dolomite or limestone bluffs occur at several places along the looping Potomac up to about Mile 86 and with the rich calcareous soil on neighboring woodland slopes support many species that are uncommon or rare in Maryland. Rocktwist, an Appalachian endemic, reaches its northernmost sites here, and snow trillium, a Midwestern species, grows at one place, the only known location for it in Maryland.

However, the south-facing slopes warm up earlier in spring and have more variety and lusher growth than the north-facing slopes. When searching for plants on any of these slopes, you should follow trails or stand at the foot of a slope and use binoculars, to avoid damaging plants.

Mile 66.9 – Lock 37.

Mile 69 – You finally emerge, from hills and mountains that began below Harpers Ferry, into the Hagerstown Valley, part of the Great Valley, which runs (geologically if not by name) from Canada to Alabama.

The careful observer might see an occasional **red-eared turtle** basking on logs among the many painted turtles. Slightly larger, it is unique among North American turtles in having a reddish stripe behind the eye. The red-ears in the canal are probably descended from released pets, as the natural range is Indiana and Alabama westward to Kansas and Texas.

Mile 69.4 – The canal crosses **Antietam Creek** on an aqueduct. This creek rises in Pennsylvania, flows past Hagerstown, and empties into the Potomac 23 miles south of Funkstown. This last stretch, especially after the I-70 crossing, makes a nice spring run by canoe or kayak through riffles and small rapids, traversing farm fields, forested hills, and the Antietam Battlefield. Antietam Creek, says Edward Gertler, "has long been a favorite for novice whitewater paddlers." One should consult a canoeing guide, such as Gertler's, before attempting any of the streams flowing down to the Potomac. They vary as to seasons, difficulty, and hazards.

Mile 69.5 – Many **osage oranges** grow in the Antietam campground. Native to Texas, Oklahoma, and Arkansas, this small, thorny tree was widely planted for hedgerows before the invention of barb wire, and it spread. It bears grapefruit-sized green seed balls. Though inedible to humans, these fruits provide food to some birds and mammals. It's one of the less bothersome exotics.

Barred Owl

Almost any night, anywhere along the canal, campers are likely to hear the loud hooting of barred owls, usually rendered as "Who cooks for you, who cooks for you-all!" Pairs may engage in antiphonal hooting, and individuals or pairs sometimes get worked up to wild cackling. Like most predatory birds, they feed on a wide variety of animal life. Mice are the mainstay, but barred owls also eat birds, insects, and other prey as large as foxes. Swamp forests are typical habitat, though they occur in other types of forest as well. Hiking on the canal, you might scare one of these big brown owls from its daytime perch in a tree, or spot one roosting in a large tree cavity, its dark eyes fixed on you as you pass.

Mile 72.7 – Lock 38. **Cliff swallows** formerly nested on piers of a Route 34 bridge across the Potomac to Shepherdstown. In 2005 there were two adjacent bridges. The swallows used the piers of the older bridge, which had an overhang at the top that protected their mud nests. The older bridge and its piers were removed later in 2005; the adaptable swallows moved to the new bridge, building about 60 nests under the concrete strip below the railing, on the downstream side of the bridge. Not restricted to cliffs, cliff swallows often nest on man-made vertical surfaces such as those on barns and bridges. Along the Potomac they are more common farther upstream in the mountains.

Five other species of swallows can be seen along the canal and river, with varying dependence on human structures for nesting. Appropriately named barn swallows usually nest in buildings or under bridges, occasionally in caves or in cliff crevices. Purple martins use various kinds of cavities but in the East rely heavily and communally on nest boxes. Tree swallows use both natural and man-made cavities, usually in trees or nest boxes. Rough-winged swallows nest in bank burrows and other cavities and niches, under bridges and wharves, in culverts and sewer pipes. Only the bank swallow, a communal nester, seems to rely entirely on "natural" sites created by nature or human digging: stream banks, gravel pits, or road cuts. This is the scarcest nesting swallow along the Potomac.

Mile 73.2-74 – Another stretch of north-facing bluffs, here formed of Conococheague limestone, provides more excellent habitat for plants. Among them are **northern white-cedars** clinging to the rock face. These are far south of their principal range in the northern states and Canada and well east of scattered populations in the Appalachians. They are probably relicts of more widespread populations during the cooler Pleistocene. Look for them, for instance, around Mile 73.5, where they are visible even when surrounding hardwoods are in full leaf. The northern white-cedar has flattened branchlets that distinguish it from eastern red cedar, which has mostly needle-like leaves and grows commonly on bluffs of all rock types, though flourishing best on limestone. Northern white-cedar can also be seen on some of the other north-facing cliffs upstream.

Mile 74 – Lock 39.

Mile 75.4 – Killiansburg Cave Hiker-Biker.

Mile 75.5-76.5 – This section, just downstream from Snyders Landing, is another notable area for **plant life**. In late April, along with Virginia bluebells and a host of other wildflowers, red-flowered erect trillium, or wakerobin, grows abundantly in the damp canal bed. It is not found growing naturally along the Potomac south of the Snyders Landing area. On the limestone bluffs grow several other species uncommon in Maryland, including northern white-cedar, walking fern, bulblet fern, and wall rue; dwarf larkspur and shooting stars bloom on top of the bluffs. Wild columbine, more common, blooms into July. Be aware that the top of the slopes around Snyders Landing are private land and require permission to enter.

There are numerous **caves** in the limestone, among them Killiansburg Cave at Mile 75.7, at the top of a slope on the berm. Actually more of a rock shelter, it is said that people hid here during the battle of Antietam. **Bats**, particularly the little brown bat and eastern pipistrelle, hibernate in some of the caves from late October to early April. Mosquitoes and flies occur near the mouth of caves; harvestmen ("daddy longlegs") and cave crickets, the latter strictly a cave species, live throughout the underground passages. Decaying organic material attracts gnats, mites, millipedes, spiders, and beetles and supports slime molds and fungi. The caves and their life, like all park resources, are protected and are not to be disturbed.

A Winter Day Around
Snyders Landing

When you get out along the canal you never know what you might see and experience. Take, for instance, a day—January 12, 1999—that I spent near Snyders Landing. From my notes:

A scene in black and white today—dark trees rising from the snow-covered ground. Dark river water flowing between white ice sheets that reach out from the shores. Smell of clean damp air, wood smoke from houses at Snyders Landing. The sound of my boots crunching on crusted snow, the cracking of ice in the river, riffles over black rocks, the raucous yelp of pileated woodpeckers.

No one had walked downstream from Snyders Landing since the snow on January 8. Tracks of dozens of squirrels and a fox crossing the towpath. The large, unmistakable three-toed tracks of wild turkeys. A fresh-cut stump indicated a winter-active beaver. A big deer bounded off through the woods. Then a mystery: on a wide shelf of ice at river's edge a dead doe lay sprawled, behind it a wide circle of blood. Possibly killed by dogs, or did someone shoot it?

The day was unusually rewarding for birds: two small groups of American pipits, a bird scarce in winter at this latitude, were finding food on ice floes, and the croak of a raven, too, was unexpected here in the middle of the Great Valley, miles from the nearest mountains. Robins—hundreds of them—were everywhere, flying over, drinking at the edge of the ice, sitting in trees.

Best of all were the waterfowl. Recent cold weather must have frozen most of the ponds and lakes in this region, sending ducks and geese to the open river. I saw fourteen species: large groups of Canada geese, black ducks, and mallards; smaller numbers of common and hooded mergansers, goldeneyes, lesser scaup, gadwalls, pintails, and shovelers; a single green-winged teal and American widgeon. A distant whiteness became, at closer range, an adult tundra swan, with an immature. Another whiteness turned out to be a snow goose.

The more you walk along the canal, the more likely you are to have a day like this.

Mile 79.4 – Lock 40.

Mile 79.7 – Horseshoe Bend Hiker-Biker.

Mile 82.7 – Big Woods Hiker-Biker. Though near Taylors Landing, this campsite, a short distance from the towpath, has a pleasantly remote feel to it. Shallow water in the canal bed sometimes attracts herons, wood ducks, and Louisiana waterthrushes. Wood ducks, which nest in tree cavities, are common and can be seen anywhere along the canal from spring to fall. In the nineteenth century they were hunted to near extinction. Full protection in the United States and Canada from 1918 to 1941 was required to bring them back. The multi-colored male is one of our most beautiful ducks. As usual among ducks, the female is drab. When pairs fly, the female emits a shrill "oo-eek!"—a good identifying sound.

The Louisiana waterthrush is actually a member of the warbler family. Living along wooded streams and ponds, it constantly bobs its tail, a common trait among streamside species.

Mile 83.3 – Dam No. 4 Cave, with a stream coming out of it in wet seasons, is on the berm in Conococheague limestone.

Mile 84 – A dry, south-facing limestone bluff bears many red cedars. Red cedars are found over much of the eastern U.S., especially on limestone soils. Most are dioecious, with male and female flowers on separate trees. The bluish, berrylike cones are relished by birds such as robins, starlings, and cedar waxwings, as well as squirrels and probably other mammals.

Mile 84.4 – A sign shows the detour route for bikers and walkers who want to continue to McMahon's Mill and beyond. The towpath between Mile 86.7 and 88.1 was eroded, overgrown, and virtually impassable. Repair and clearance may be completed by 2011 or earlier, so canal travelers can return to this route.

Mile 84.6 – Twenty-foot-high Dam No. 4 backs water up for 13 1/2 miles, in the Big Slackwater.

Mile 85.6-86.7 – In this stretch are occasional limestone bluffs, first of the Rockdale Run Formation and then of the Stonehenge Formation. At Mile 86.7 you must backtrack unless the work described above (Mile 84.4) has been completed.

Mile 88.1 – Three-mile-long Downey Branch reaches the river here and once powered McMahon's Mill, still standing. Much watercress grows upstream in Downey Branch, indicating spring sources of the water. This plant, now so widespread in cool waters across America, was introduced from Europe.

Mile 88.3 – A stream issues from Howell Cave in a dark gray limestone cliff. The opening is very small and a sign warns: "Danger. Keep Out."

Mile 88.3-88.9 – Cliffs of dark gray to black limestone of the Rockdale Formation.

Mile 88.9 – Lock 41, followed by **Lock 42** at Mile 89.

Mile 89.4-89.9 – The canal and berm area have become a wooded swamp, home of wood ducks and barred owls.

Mile 90.8 – Opequon Junction Hiker-Biker.

Dragonflies

Dragonflies live mostly around water; thus the canal and river sport many of these fast-flying, colorful predators. They feed mostly on insects, from flies and midges to other dragonflies, moths, and butterflies, but one species has been known to catch hummingbirds! They lay their eggs in water, bottom sediment, or on aquatic plants. The larvae live underwater, eating aquatic insects and larger animals to the size of tadpoles and small fish. After 8 to 17 sheddings of their exoskeleton they crawl from the water and metamorphose into winged adults. Along the canal, some of the most common species are the common whitetail (*Libellula Lydia,* illustrated here), which has a thick, chalky white abdomen and broad black bands across the wings; the blue dasher (*Pachydiplax longipennis*), smaller, with blue, black-tipped abdomen, and often amber patches in the wings; the eastern pondhawk (*Erythemis simplicicollis*), with powdery blue abdomen and thorax and clear wings; and the swamp darner (*Epiaeschna heros*), huge, with dark brown abdomen banded with green rings and clear or amber-tinged wings. (These are descriptions of males. The female swamp darner is similar to the male; females of the other species have brown or greenish abdomens with yellowish bands or stripes.) The closely related damselflies are usually smaller and hold their wings pressed together over their backs or partially spread, while dragonflies hold their wings straight out to the sides. (See Nikula and Sones 2002 for identification of common species.)

Photo by Connie Durnan.

Mile 92-95 – Bluffs of Chambersburg limestone. A lovely stream—perhaps seasonal—tumbles over rock ledges on the berm at Mile 92.2.

Mile 92.9 – Lock 43.

Mile 95.2 – Cumberland Valley Hiker-Biker.

Mile 95.4 – Outcrops of Martinsburg shale occur here and between Miles 95.5 and 95.7.

Mile 98.9-99.6 – The canal is watered up to the **Conococheague Aqueduct** and **Cushwa loading basin**, a popular fishing place at the foot of Williamsport, and site of the NPS Williamsport Visitor Center. The visitor center has exhibits about life on the canal and books for sale. An arrow on the first-floor wall points to the 1996 flood level, about five feet above the floor. The 1936 flood reached the second floor.

At **Mile 99.2** you pass the huge Allegheny Power Plant, a coal-fired steam-electric plant. **Conococheague Creek** begins on South Mountain in Pennsylvania and flows through scenic farmland to the Potomac. Some 71 miles of it are described by Gertler as canoeable.

Mile 99.1 – Lock 44.

Mile 100.5 – A sewage treatment plant lies beyond concrete steps up the berm slope.

Mile 101.2 – Jordan Junction Hiker-Biker.

Mile 102.2 – Beyond a gap in cliffs on the berm is the **Pinesburg limestone quarry**.

Mile 102.3-110.2 – Occasional limestone bluffs, up to 100 feet high.

Mile 105.5 – In June 2005 I encountered a **wood turtle** on the towpath here. I mention this just because this is near the southern edge of this scarce species's range, which extends north to New Brunswick and west to the upper Great Lakes. It has a "sculptured" shell, somewhat flatter than that of the more common eastern box turtle, which ranges from southern Pennsylvania and Massachusetts to Georgia.

Mile 106 – You can hear **Little Conococheague Creek** splashing over rocks on the berm. A short walk across the grassy canal bed gives a nice view up the wooded stream, which rises on Bear Pond Mountain, just across the Pennsylvania line. **Rough-winged swallows** nest in the river end of the stone culvert. This is the swallow most often seen along the river in summer. Drabbest of the swallows, it is gray-brown above and dull white below.

Mile 106.6 – Twenty-foot-high **Dam No. 5** creates seven miles of slackwater above it. From here to Hancock, much multiflora rose and Japanese honeysuckle is blooming in June. Though exotic species, they are pretty, and honeysuckle, of course, smells good.

Mile 107 – Lock 45.

Mile 107.2 – Lock 46.

Mile 108.8-109 – Four Locks (Locks 47-50). The canal cuts across **Praether's Neck** rather than following the long loop of the river. The park service is acquiring pieces of the 1000-acre neck as they become available, which will eventually form another large node of the mostly narrow canal park.

Mile 109 – Low outcrops of limestone rise along the river side of the towpath in this area.

Mile 109.6 – North Mountain Hiker-Biker.

Mile 110.2 – McCoys Ferry Recreation Area offers drive-in camping. Limestone bluffs end here. Lowland forest dominates the next 14 miles to Hancock. Nearby shale and sandstone outcrops signal a shift in geology—leaving the limestone-dolomite country—as the mountains are approached.

About one and a half miles long, Big Pool is a popular fishing place and a stopover spot for migrating waterbirds.

Mile 111.5 – One begins seeing signs on the river side of the towpath announcing **Fort Frederick State Park**. The fort, now reconstructed, was built in 1756 during the French and Indian Wars.

Mile 112.1 – The state park road crosses the towpath on its way to a campground by the river, under tall silver maples. Beaver ponds on the river side of the towpath attract nesting Canada geese, wood ducks, and prothonotary warblers.

The canal widens here into **Big Pool**, a marsh that canal engineers turned into a 1.6-mile-long lake. Anglers fish it for smallmouth bass, bluegills, and rainbow trout, the latter of which the Maryland DNR stocks every spring for a "put-and-take" fishery. Big Pool is sometimes a good place to see migrating waterfowl and loons. Beaver cuttings are frequent along the shore.

The paved **Western Maryland Rail Trail**, which runs from Fort Frederick to Pearre (Mile 136.2), begins one-half mile north of the park entrance, beside Route 56. This is the edge of mountain country, and bikers occasionally see **black bears** along the trail, a possibility that also exists along the canal up to Cumberland.

Mile 112.5-117.8 – Fields, some in hay or corn, some fallow, lie along the river side of the towpath for much of this stretch. The field from about Mile 113 to 113.9 often has rain pools in spring that attract **migrating shorebirds**, especially solitary sandpipers and lesser yellowlegs.

Alexander Wetmore, ornithologist and former Secretary of the Smithsonian Institution, stated that going upriver one first encounters breeding **black-capped chickadees** around Big Pool. The *Atlas of the Breeding Birds of Maryland and the District of Columbia* (1996) shows both the northerly black-capped and southerly Carolina chickadee in this general area. Telling them apart is tricky, and hybrids may occur, but it's interesting to try to make the separation as you progress up the canal. The black-capped is slightly larger, with entirely white cheek patch, a more distinct white wing stripe with a "hockey-blade" end, and a slower, lower call. Bird banders say that blackcaps have a noticeably larger head.

Mile 113.7 – The upper end of Big Pool: Look for tree swallows nesting in cavities of dead trees and green herons here and in the swamp on the river side of the towpath. At low water levels, the mud flats on the Big Pool shore sometimes attract migrating shorebirds.

Traffic noise on nearby I-70 from here to Mile 122.5 somewhat diminishes the pleasure of this next section.

Mile 116 – Licking Creek Hiker Biker.

Mile 116.1 – Licking Creek Aqueduct. Licking Creek begins on the west slope of Tuscarora Mountain, well up in Pennsylvania. The lower 45 miles of it are suitable for novice paddlers and wind through scenic farm and mountain country. Water levels are adequate in winter and spring within 24 hours after a hard rain.

Mile 120.2-120.9 – Little Pool, a lovely smaller edition of Big Pool, offers a view upstream of a distant mountain ridge. Below the bridge at the downstream end note the white-flowered lizard's tail, which blooms from June to September. In the upper end are patches of spatterdock, with its large leaves rising out of the water and globular yellow flowers from May to October.

Mile 120.7 – Little Pool Hiker-Biker is a pleasant place to camp and enjoy its namesake.

Mile 121.7 – Ditch Run passes under the canal.

Mile 122.7 – Lock 51.

Mile 122.9 – Lock 52.

Lizard's tail, a common plant in swamps and shallow water. *Photo by Connie Durnan.*

Mile 123 – Tonoloway Creek Aqueduct. Tonoloway Creek drains an area east of Sideling Hill. The last 21 miles or so, which have strong current but easy riffles, are suitable for novice paddlers, within a day or two of hard rain. According to Gertler, "almost every bend exposes pretty shale cliffs, and almost every northern exposure displays a cool green hemlock grove."

Mile 124.1-124.4 – This section of the canal is watered, attracting anglers. **Little Tonoloway Recreation Area,** at Mile 124.4, has a picnic area and boat ramp. Just beyond it, the towpath passes over **Little Tonoloway Creek**, which rises on Sideling Hill, to the west, and has tributaries coming in from nearby Pennsylvania, to the north. **Hancock**, on the berm, is one of the larger towns along the canal. The park service's Hancock Visitor Center is at the east end, down a side road to the left as you enter the town on MD 144.

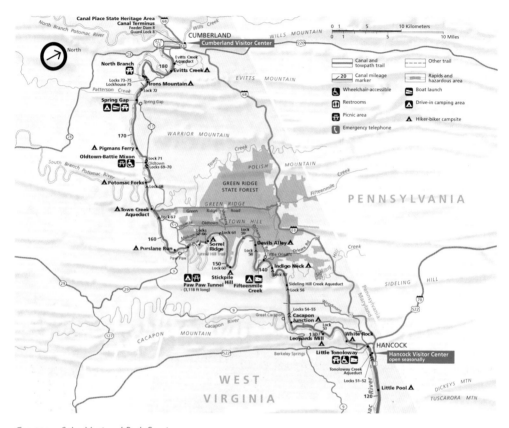

Courtesy of the National Park Service.

Hancock to Cumberland

This is the wildest part of the canal, cutting through one forested ridge after another. Sighting a bear is possible, although not probable, and even a mountain lion is remotely possible. A highlight is the Paw Paw Tunnel, dug through a shale ridge, upon which rare shale barren plants grow. The last few miles—much of it passing farms and residential areas—presage the urban end at Cumberland.

Mile 126.2 – An old **apple orchard** flanks the canal on the berm. It appears disused, but apple-growing is still important around Hancock.

Mile 126.4 – White Rock Hiker-Biker is named for the high cliff across the river, a likely nesting spot for ravens.

Mile 127 – In the small outcrop of white Keefer sandstone on the berm, small **crinoid fossils** of the Silurian era are common. From here to the canal terminus at Cumberland, almost all of the rock outcrops are sandstone or shale of the Devonian era, 345-405 million years ago. In keeping with the general progression of younger rocks up the Potomac, these are younger than the Cambrian, Ordovician, and Silurian limestone and dolomite of the Great Valley, and older than the Permian and Pennsylvanian strata encountered beyond Cumberland. Some formations, like the one here, contain fossils, and these, like the rocks themselves, must be left in place.

Layers of sandstone and shale, an anticline, form the Devil's Eyebrow, near a former lime kiln. *Photo by Connie Durnan.*

Mile 127.3 – A prominent anticline on the berm forms the **Devil's Eyebrow**, composed of red sandstone, red shale, and some green shale of the Bloomsburg Formation. It arches over a small cave, the "eye." Red cedars grow atop the Eyebrow. Just upstream are eight stone arches of a lime kiln, which was supplied with limestone from tunnels in the hillside. And just beyond that are the brick remains of the Round Top Hydraulic Cement Mill, which operated from 1838 to 1909.

Mile 128 – Beyond Roundtop Hill the canal passes through a flat wooded valley. Now in the Valley and Ridge Province, one sees a sequence of mountain ridges alternating with wooded valleys and hills.

Mile 128.7 – An old beaver pond with shallow water extends upstream for about 3/4 mile. Remains of a beaver lodge can be seen on the berm. Beavers almost always have built their lodges on the berm, perhaps to distance themselves from human traffic on the towpath. A small stream enters the pond at the upper end, providing the water that was dammed farther down.

Mile 130 – Leopards Mill Hiker-Biker.

Mile 130.1 – Lock 53.

Mile 130.8 – Cohill Station, a road access point.

Mile 132.9 – The symmetrical anticline in Keefer sandstone is known as the Devil's Eyebrow (in addition to the better known site at Mile 127.3).

Mile 133.7 – Cacapon Junction Hiker-Biker, named for the mouth of the Cacapon River, directly across the Potomac. This is a popular stream with canoeists and kayakers comfortable in white water.

Mile 134 – Lock 54. The river cuts through **Tonoloway Ridge**, clearly seen beyond the berm.

Mile 134.2 – Lock 55. The remains of Dam No. 6 extend into the river.

Mile 136.2 – Lock 56, at **Pearre**, locally pronounced PA-ree. This is the present upstream terminus of the Western Maryland Rail Trail, which parallels the canal from Fort Frederick State Park.

Mile 136.6 – Sideling Hill Creek Aqueduct. Sideling Hill Creek, which rises in Bedford County, Pennsylvania, is described by Edward Gertler as the best canoe/kayak run on the Potomac tributaries in the Maryland Valley and Ridge Province. He says the upper section passes "mostly through woods filled with hemlock and rhododendron," and the lower section "is an almost wild river." It's canoeable in winter and spring after two to four days of hard rain.

Near the mouth of Sideling Hill Creek, scour bars in the river, according to Steve Wiegand, a Maryland DNR botanist, produce "an incredible display of flowers in summer." During low water one can walk onto these bars.

Mile 139.4 – Lock 57.

Mile 139.5 – Indigo Neck Hiker-Biker. Indigo Neck is a remote area where two park service maintenance men reported seeing a **mountain lion**. At least two other sightings have been reported between Hancock and Little Orleans (just upstream). One was of a mother and two cubs, indicating a truly wild animal (or of a released pet now established in the wild). However, scientists tend to

Duckweed

The bright green covering you see in shallow water in much of the canal is duckweed, and probably the common, widespread "least duckweed." This is an unusual little organism, different in form and habit from most flowering plants. Look closely and you can distinguish tiny individuals, with three fronds surrounded by a leaf-like structure called a spathe. The roundish fronds are only 2-5 mm in diameter and have slender rootlets dangling beneath, though the plant is free-floating. It sometimes produces miniscule flowers and then seeds, but most reproduction occurs through fronds detaching from mother fronds, and those daughter fronds producing daughters. This species lives only five to six weeks, but reproduces rapidly. Least duckweed, like other duckweeds, can flourish in water that is full of organic impurities. The duckweeds presumably get their name from the fact that waterfowl eat them.

Photos by Connie Durnan.

disbelieve these mountain lion reports, since none have been shot by hunters or found dead on the roads in this region. The subject of mountain lions in eastern North America has produced two camps: many dubious scientists versus other people who are sure they've seen the big cats with the long tails. Sightings have increased in the Midwest, suggesting possible eastward wandering of animals from their strongholds in the West. If some in the East are released pets, the question is, can they reproduce and form established populations? It seems definite that many reports are correct identifications.

Mile 140.9 – Fifteen Mile Creek Riverside Park (camping) and **Little Orleans**. I have seen **bald eagles** three times around Little Orleans (spring—a pair, summer, and winter) and suspect they nest in the area. The Maryland DNR, when conducting flights to check on eagle's nests, did not go beyond Harpers Ferry and have discontinued these flights now because of the extent of eagle recovery. Nests are known on the South Branch of the Potomac in West Virginia, and probably there are some upstream from Harpers Ferry.

Bill Schoenadel, proprietor of the store and restaurant at Little Orleans since 1969, is a great source of information about local fish and wildlife (including the mountain lion and cubs mentioned above, bears, etc.), though perhaps prone to exaggeration, according to one scientist.

An aqueduct carries the canal over **Fifteen Mile Creek**, which drains the shaley ridges of Buchanan State Forest in Pennsylvania and Green Ridge State Forest in Maryland (see Side Trip: Green Ridge State Forest). About 10 miles of the lower section, through Green Ridge State Forest, is canoeable after hard rain in winter or spring, but with sharp bends and fallen trees, plus fast water, which require skill from boaters.

Mile 141.3-143.6 – Rock strata on the dry hillsides are found at all angles, up to nearly vertical. These strata are mostly dark gray sandstone of the Catskill Formation. The materials that became sedimentary rock were, of course, laid down horizontally, and the resulting rock was folded when tectonic plates collided and formed the Appalachians. Farther west, on the Allegheny Plateau, where the pressure was much less, you can see (along highways such as I-68) that the strata are nearly level.

Mile 143.6 – An old beaver dam backs water up to Mile 144, forming a long, wide pond.

Mile 144 – Lock 58. A sign shows trails in **Green Ridge State Forest**, one of which (the Long Pond Red Trail) begins here. This is part of an 18-mile trail loop that returns to the canal at Lock 67 (see Side Trip: Green Ridge State Forest).

Mile 144.5 – Devils Alley Hiker-Biker.

Mile 144.7 – A high outcrop is topped by Virginia pines. The dark gray to black sandstone has thin veins of calcite. Geologist William Davies wrote, in his detailed manuscript, *The Geology and Engineering Structures of the Chesapeake and Ohio Canal*, that the beds form a tightly folded syncline, "one of the few that are well exposed along the canal."

Spiders

It's too bad that so many people dislike or fear spiders. They are well worth looking at and studying for their great diversity of appearance and ways of living. Some 3,500 species have been described in North America. In early fall along the canal the large webs of orb-weavers, such as the black and yellow argiope illustrated here, become conspicuous, as individuals grow to their largest size, the owner often sitting in the middle waiting for prey to hit the web. Other groups of spiders have different habits. Some spin webs, others don't. Jumping spiders, all of which are small and most are brightly colored, leap on their prey. If they miss their mark they can crawl back along a silk thread they secured at the leap-off point. Wolf spiders run on the ground and rest under stones or in burrows. They constitute many of the Arctic and high mountain species. Crab spiders hold their legs crab-like, out at the sides, and can walk forwards, sideways, and backward. They ambush their prey. Some sit on flowers, waiting for an insect to arrive. Many spiders are difficult to identify, but a good introduction to representative species and their behavior is the *Golden Guide, Spiders and Their Kin,* by Levi and Levi, 2002.

Photo by Connie Durnan.

Mile 146.5 – Lock 59.

Mile 147-148.7 – This is an attractive area for wildlife (e.g., a variety of sparrows in winter), with fallow fields on the river side, a marshy strip adjacent to the towpath part of the way, and a beaver pond extending upstream from a dam at Mile 147.1 for about a half-mile. Then the forest closes in again. The moderate size of trees here suggests this too was farm fields 75-100 years ago.

Mile 149.3 – Stickpile Hill Hiker-Biker.

Mile 149.6 – Lock 60.

Mile 150.1 – An access road from Kasecamp Road crosses the towpath on its way to a riverside picnic area and boat ramp, on Green Ridge State Forest land. Though there are a few houses on Kasecamp Road, this area has a nice remote feel to it.

Mile 151-151.7 – Shallow water in the canal, as at many other such places, provides habitat for turtles, muskrats, wood ducks, herons, dragonflies, and other life. Many Virginia pines and red cedars grow on the flanking dry hills.

Mile 152 – The high bluff on the berm is composed of gray shale and sandstone of the Chemung Formation.

Mile 153.1 – Lock 61.

Mile 154.2 – Sorrel Ridge Hiker-Biker and **Lock 62**. In 1999, and perhaps later, there was a lovely beaver pond between here and the next lock. This is now drained and is filled with meadow-like vegetation.

Mile 154.5 – Lock 63 1/3. The strange numbering is due to the fact that the canal company found that one less lock was needed here than planned, and locks farther upstream had already been numbered in contracts. The unusual numbering was supposed to cover up the difference; but still there is no Lock 65 and I wonder why they bothered with the fractions.

Mile 154.6 – Lock 64 2/3. On the way up to the Paw Paw Tunnel, the slope on your left faces north and the slope on your right faces south. Most of the pines on the cooler north-facing slope are white pines, and on the hot, dry south-facing slope are Virginia pines, because of differing adaptations to the opposing environments. The appearance of long-needled white pines upstream from Hancock (as well as increased incidence of sugar maple) is an indicator of cooler conditions in the mountains.

Mile 154.7 – Lock 66.

Mile 154.8 – The 2-mile **Tunnel Hill Trail** leaves the towpath and goes over this hill, reconnecting with the towpath at the upstream portal of the Paw Paw Tunnel. This trail traverses terrain that is very different from the flood plain woods you see along most of the towpath. Instead of sycamore, silver maple, and box elder, you find on Tunnel Hill a rather dry forest of oaks and pines, hickory, and red maple. Instead of spicebush and paw paw, mountain laurel and huckleberry are prominent in the shrub layer. Spring wildflowers include trailing arbutus and the two-toned bird's-foot violet. Descending on the upriver side, you pass a small patch of shale barren, where plants restricted to this habitat grow (see Side Trip: Green Ridge State Forest). Ahead, you get a magnificent view of the winding river, fields and forests, and the mountains beyond.

Smooth shale "slickensides" near the Paw Paw Tunnel were pinned down by square iron plates to prevent the thin layers from sliding down onto the towpath and canal. *Photos by Connie Durnan.*

Mile 155 – The towpath becomes a boardwalk to the tunnel entrance. You are now in a deep ravine, cut through shale by the canal builders. Beside you, on the left, "**slickensides**," smooth surfaces where one bed of shale has moved over another, slope steeply down. These beds have been pinned with iron rods capped by square plates to prevent slippage, but on the berm they haven't been secured. There, piles of thin shale fragments have accumulated at the foot of the cut.

The red-spotted newt and tadpoles (above) can be seen in the shallow water outside the downstream portal of the Paw Paw Tunnel. *Photo by Connie Durnan.*

Springs in the tunnel maintain a year-round flow of clear, shallow water, where hundreds of tiny fish feed outside the tunnel. Look also for red-spotted newts, tadpoles, and water snakes. On a hot day, the cool air issuing from the tunnel is delightfully refreshing.

Mile 155.2 – The north (but downstream) portal of the Paw Paw Tunnel. A flashlight is recommended for the 3,118-foot passage, which gets pretty dark in the middle. A railing on the canal side of the towpath helps anyone without a flashlight to feel their way.

Mile 155.8 – A small picnic area is situated just outside the south portal of the tunnel.

Mile 156.2 – The canal goes under Route 51.

Mile 156.9 – Purslane Run Hiker-Biker.

Mile 157.3 – Purslane Run passes under the canal. It begins a few miles away on Town Hill.

Mile 161.7 – Lock 67. A metal post with a hiking symbol in the canal bed shows an entrance to the Green Ridge Hiking Trail, which loops for 18 miles through Green Ridge State Forest. (See Side Trip: Green Ridge State Forest.)

Mile 162 – Town Creek Hiker-Biker.

Mile 162.4 – Town Creek Aqueduct. Town Creek begins in the middle of Bedford County, Pennsylvania, and winds through a sparsely inhabited valley in the mountains in its upper section, and through less remote, less mountainous country south of I-68. Gertler describes it as canoeable in winter or spring after hard rain.

Mile 162.4-164.8 – I find this stretch's natural features especially attractive. The canal is wide and watered. Steep forested hills rise on the berm. On the river side, a strip of cattail marsh parallels the canal, and beyond that are fallow fields and cropland. I've seen here a big herd of deer, a red fox, a mink hunting along Town Creek, and a bald eagle flying over.

The watered section of the canal extends from Town Creek to mile 167.2, above Oldtown.

Mile 163.7 – A dramatic outcrop, especially striking in morning sunlight, projects from the berm hillside amid Virginia pines and red cedars.

Mile 164.8 – Lock 68 and the **Potomac Forks Hiker-Biker**. The name refers to the nearby junction of the South Branch with the North Branch.

Mile 165 – A long ledge of bluish Ridgeley sandstone backed by a dense stand of Virginia pine runs along the berm for about 0.4 miles. At the downstream end of this outcrop is a big patch of **rosebay rhododendron** (*Rhododendron maximum*), with smaller patches along the outcrop. This large evergreen shrub, most common in the southern Appalachians, blooms in June and July.

One winter I saw otter tracks in the snow here, ascending from the river and entering the canal. Farther downstream I'd seen tracks of two otters in the towpath, an otter slide, holes in the ice where one had come up or dove, and blood and fish scales on the bank. The Maryland DNR released otters on several tributary streams of the Potomac in Allegany County in the mid-1980s and now they occur along much of the upper Potomac, and nearly state-wide from other releases.

River Otters

Though scattered along much of the Potomac, otters are wary and seldom seen. They are engaging animals, with a love of play. They especially enjoy sliding down snowy banks or bare banks into water. But they are also ferocious predators. A wildlife biologist of my acquaintance with extensive knowledge of the species calls them "water wolves." They eat everything from snails and clams to suckers, muskrats, and ducks, though they favor crayfish in summer and fish in winter. This puts them at odds with aquaculturists and some anglers. They usually make their home in a bank burrow, perhaps an enlarged muskrat or beaver den, after the previous owner has departed or been killed. In these burrows, the one to five, usually two or three, pups are born in April. After years of rarity, the otter, fortunately, is once again an established member of the Potomac valley ecosystem.

Mile 165.5 – Here one sees fields in a rare pocket of level land a half mile wide and more than a mile long. This opening in the hills was exploited by Indians for many centuries. Groups lived and traded here, at the meeting place of several trails. In 1692 Shawnees established a village. When the first white settler, Colonel Thomas Cresap, arrived about 1740, the place was known as Shawnee Old Town; a few years later it became simply **Oldtown**, and today is a small settlement that flanks the canal for a mile or so.

Mile 166.5 – Lock 69.

Mile 166.7 – Lock 70.

Mile 167 – Lock 71.

Mile 167.2 – A dam across the canal ponds water above it. From here at least to Mile 173 is beaver exhibit A, with lodges, dams, and cuttings.

Mile 167.5 – The canal runs through a deep cut in Marcellus shale. Piles of the sharp flakes edge the towpath and may present a hazard to bicycle tires. The shaley slopes support drought-resistant trees such as chestnut oak and Virginia pine.

One of many beaver lodges upstream from Oldtown. *Photo by Connie Durnan.*

Beds and fragments of Marcellus shale in a cut made for the canal and towpath.

Beavers have created this large, spadderdock-filled pond by building and maintaining dams at the upstream and downstream ends. *Photos by Connie Durnan.*

Mile 168.4 – A lovely, wide pond with spatterdock—note the yellow, ball-like flowers—has been created by two-foot-high beaver dams at either end. On the berm are more shaley slopes covered with Virginia pines.

Mile 168.6 – A 60-foot bluff of dark gray Mahantango shale rises on the berm.

Mile 168.8-171 – Fields stretch along the river side. Water in the canal provided by beaver dams, a few marshy strips along the river side of the towpath, the fields, and some woods, make for habitat and scenic variety. Around Mile 169.6 look for deer tracks where these animals cross a beaver dam to get to and from farm fields when the water is too deep for easy crossing elsewhere.

Mile 169.1 – **Pigmans Ferry Hiker-Biker** is near the towpath but far from the river.

Mile 171.9 – Thin rock layers on the berm form a small symmetrical anticline.

Mile 172.9 – A sandstone bluff up to 60 feet high sports a surprisingly varied botanical mix: white, pitch, and Virginia pines, hemlock, red cedar, mountain laurel, and a big patch of rosebay rhododendron. With binoculars, botanists might spot some interesting plants on the mossy cliff face.

Mile 173.3 – **Spring Gap Recreation Area**, shaded by tall cottonwoods, silver maples, and sycamores, offers drive-in camping and a boat ramp.

Mile 173.6 – **Colliers Run**, which passes under the canal, begins near Rocky Gap State Park on the west flank of Martin Mountain.

Mile 174.3 – An obscure trail on the river side 100 yards downstream from Lock 72 leads to **Blue Spring**. This unprepossessing upwelling has been described as one of the largest springs in eastern North America. On my first visit here in the 1970s, Jim Paulus, a naturalist who lived in Oldtown, pointed out carp, fallfish, sunfish, chain pickerel, white sucker, smallmouth bass, and other fish in the clear water. Jim said it turns milky blue when the river is high.

Mile 174.4 – **Lock 72**. Here the canal squeezes between Irons Mountain and the river at what was known as The Narrows. From here to Cumberland the landscape opens up as the canal follows three giant bends of the river. Farms and residential areas alternate with wooded patches.

Mile 175.4 – **Lock 73** and **Irons Mountain Hiker-Biker**.

Mile 175.5 – **Lock 74** and the **North Branch Recreation Area,** for drive-in picnicking.

Mile 175.7 – **Lock 75**, the last lift lock on the canal.

Mile 176 – The **North Branch Sewage Pumping Station**, also identified as the Mexico Farms Pretreatment Facility, lies on the river side. The covered sewage lagoons once were open and treated waste from a Pittsburgh Plate Glass Company plant. Jim Paulus, an avid birder, worked for PPG and frequently checked these lagoons. He recorded a surprising variety of waterbirds, including some you wouldn't expect up here in the mountains, such as the ruddy turnstone, a shorebird.

Mile 176.5 – Past a large farm, you can look out over a wide expanse of marshy land with bare patches, where sprinklers used to periodically spray water. This was effluent from the Fibred Company plant on the berm. The spray apparently killed the vegetation around the sprinklers.

The humpy hilltops of **Knobly Mountain** can be seen to the west. The area within this river bend, known as Mexico Farms, lies on a huge terrace 125 feet above the river. Like other such terraces, it is covered with river gravel below the soil.

Mile 177.9 – A huge **swamp white oak** grows here next to a horse pasture. A former plaque at the site called it the Maryland State Champion of this species, with circumference at 4 feet above the ground of 16 feet, 2 inches.

Mile 180 – **Evitts Creek Hiker-Biker**, the last campsite before Cumberland. Situated on a terrace along the river, it looks across the canal to the CSX railroad yards, which stretch for over a mile toward Cumberland. Adjacent power lines cross the river, where lies a more bucolic scene of farm fields.

Mile 180.7 – Evitts Creek Aqueduct. Evitts Creek winds down from Bedford County, Pennsylvania. One tributary, Rocky Gap Run, has been dammed to form Lake Habeeb at Rocky Gap State Park.

Mile 181.2-181.6 – The canal bed is cattail marsh, a scarce habitat along the canal, up to 60 yards wide. It's full of red-winged blackbirds in season and a good hangout for green herons.

Mile 181.8 – On the river side are the **Cumberland Waste Water Treatment Plant** and grassy fields of the **Riverside Recreation Area**. All of Cumberland's waste water does not reach this plant, as there are at least three Combined Sewage Overflow outlets to the river at Cumberland for times of high flow.

Mile 182.6 – A well-constructed beaver dam and another 0.2 mile upstream form a (probably active) beaver pond, with lodges.

Spring migrating waterfowl often rest on this section of the Potomac's North Branch below Cumberland.

Mile 183.5 – The canal emerges from trees and one sees ahead the church spires of **Cumberland**. River overflow pools attract shorebirds such as solitary sandpipers in spring. The river from here to the canal terminus often has waterfowl, locally resident Canada geese and mallards and sometimes migrants in spring that put down perhaps because they see the urban area ahead.

Mile 184.5 – **Terminus of the C & O Canal**. The boardwalk to your right leads to the Cumberland NPS Visitor Center on the first floor of the renovated Western Maryland Railway Station. This visitor center has the most extensive, and very well done, exhibits of the NPS centers along the canal. They portray canal operations, canal boat construction, coal mining, the changing Cumberland area economy, and other aspects of canal and Cumberland life. Ambitious bicyclists can continue past the railway station all the way to Pittsburgh on the Cumberland and Pittsburgh bike trail.

In June 2010 at least two pairs of **cliff swallows** were nesting on the I-68 highway bridge at the Western Maryland Railway Station.

Side Trip: Green Ridge State Forest

Green Ridge State Forest, upstream from Little Orleans, spreads over 43,000 acres of mountain forest adjacent to the canal. Here you can walk dry ridges up to 2,000 feet in elevation and moist stream valleys, see a few of the more northerly plants and animals, and explore shale barrens, an environment unique to the central Appalachians. A multiple-use area, Green Ridge is managed primarily for recreation, such as camping, hunting, and even off-road vehicle (ORV) riding, on a trail that loops through the center of the Forest, but also for timber harvesting on many areas and forest preservation on others. The result is an interesting mosaic of environments in different stages of succession.

Beginning at Lock 58 (Mile 144), the canal passes through the state forest for most of the next 18 miles. Foot access via roads and trails can be gained at Lock 58 (Mile 144), Mile 147.4, Bond's Landing (Mile 150), Mile 153.3, Malcolm Road, which crosses the trail over the Paw Paw Tunnel hill, and at Lock 67 (Mile 161.7).

An 18-mile loop trail through Green Ridge State Forest here passes through a hemlock grove beside Deep Run.

Along Deep Run, with its large hemlocks, white pines, and other "cove hardwood" trees, a person can enjoy one of the loveliest parts of Green Ridge State Forest. *Photo by Connie Durnan.*

The Green Ridge Hiking Trail departs the towpath at Lock 58 and returns to it at Lock 67. This trail winds uphill for several miles, then follows Fifteen Mile Creek, Deep Run, and Big Run for about 10 miles, and finally descends to the canal along the slopes of Green Ridge. Camping is allowed anywhere along this trail and at three Adirondack shelters, with a permit. In total, the loop is 18 miles. Serious long-distance hikers have an option of taking the Pine Lick Blue Trail, which branches off from the Green Ridge Hiking Trail, goes north 6 miles to the Pennsylvania line, and connects with trails in that state. Many lightly-traveled dirt roads that wind through the state forest also make pleasant walking. Campers can also drive from I-68 at 15-Mile Creek into any of the 115 primitive campsites (picnic table only) scattered through the forest.

Only the most discerning eye would guess the history of these forested ridges. For several decades after 1829, the William Carroll /Richard Caton venture cut timber, mined iron ore, and attempted iron manufacture. However, the canal that they counted on to ship out timber was not in full operation until the second half of the century; the iron ore was scanty, and iron manufacturing failed. A chimney from Carroll's steam-powered sawmill still stands beside Carroll Road.

More intensive exploitation began in the 1880s. Between 1880 and 1914 logging companies cut over most of the area. Fires, which followed much of the early logging in North America, reportedly ensued here as well. The next venture was an apple orchard development in the early part of the twentieth century. Orchard companies bought some 45,000 acres and subdivided the area into ten-acre parcels. These were sold as investment and retirement properties. Five acres of each were cleared, burned, and planted in apple trees. The best timber on the other five acres was cut. This scheme eventually failed and the interests of the last corporation were acquired by the State Department of Forestry in 1931. Green Ridge State Forest began then with around 14,400 acres.

At one time there were 3,000 owners of these ten-acre parcels. Today, some 250 remain in private hands, most used as hunting camps or vacation home-sites. A couple of farms not bought by the orchard companies are still privately owned as well. Forest has regrown on most of the land, with canopy trees mostly 90 to 100 years old. On dry, steep shale barrens, where growth is slow, trees are small but some are more than 200 years old. Oaks – white, red, chestnut, black, scarlet, and post – predominate in the state forest. Mixed in are red maple, tulip tree, black gum, hickories, and others, with white pine on moister slopes and Virginia pine, a successional species now fading, on ridges and drier slopes. The stream-valley forests appeal to me the most. Cool moist habitats here support big hemlocks and white pines up to 2 feet or more in diameter, sugar maples, basswood, white ash, black walnut, and other "cove hardwood" species.

Green Ridge State Forest is divided into three management zones. No timber cutting is allowed on Water Management Zones and Special Management Zones, which encompass about 40 percent of the state forest. These protect stream courses, valleys, and other areas of high natural value. Timber cutting is allowed on the other 60 percent—General Management Zones. This was formerly typical clear-cutting, but now certain trees are left standing, such as snags (dead trees), uncommon species, especially good specimens of common species, and all white pines and hickories. A roughly 100-year rotation is followed, meaning that a given area is cut only every 100 years or so. The general result is a patchwork of stands of different ages, although most of what one sees along roads looks like well developed forest. Early successional stages and old growth occupy much less area than intermediate stands.

The cutting is done partly to benefit wildlife, much of which uses open, brushy areas, as well as closed forest. Deer and wild turkeys abound, much to the delight of the numerous hunters in season. Ruffed grouse and squirrels (gray, fox, and red) occupy the next echelon of hunting attention. Bobcats live here and occasionally a black bear is spotted.

Naturalists may be especially interested in the more northerly species found here, and in exploring the shale barrens. Among trees, white pine, hemlock, black birch, yellow birch (a few), and striped maple (a small tree) fall in the northerly category. Among birds, the following were found in the breeding season during work on the first Maryland Breeding Bird Atlas (1996): ruffed grouse, black-billed cuckoo, black-capped chickadee, blue-headed vireo, golden-winged, Nashville, chestnut-sided, and black –throated green warblers, and rose-breasted grosbeak. The mammals of northerly distribution include masked shrew, red squirrel, red-backed vole, and woodland jumping mouse. Among the reptiles and amphibians, wood turtles occur here, though uncommonly. Two snakes to be aware of: copperhead and timber rattlesnake. The rattlesnake is uncommon. "Thank goodness," says the ordinary citizen. "Unfortunately," says the naturalist, who is interested in all native life.

Shale barrens are probably the most distinctive environment of Green Ridge. Usually steep, and baking in summer, they appeal mostly to botanists. They occur on south- or southwest-facing slopes where weathered shale chips have slid down and covered the surface of the soil. Many plants cannot tolerate the hot, dry conditions that result, and of those that can, some are endemic—found only on shale barrens.

Kates Mountain clover, a shale barren plant of the Central Appalachians. *Photo by Robert Johnsson, courtesy of Fanny Johnsson.*

Green Ridge State Forest has many patches of shale barren. In late June 2001, Bob and Fanny Johnsson took me to three of the more accessible sites to hunt for the endemics. Beside Picklick Road, just off Fifteen Mile Creek Road, we found shale barren morning glory; shale barren pussytoes; *Paronychia fastigiata*, with its tiny linear leaves and tiny pale lavender flowers; and Kates Mountain clover, a strict shale barren endemic. This clover received its name from the locality in West Virginia where it was first discovered. Kates Mountain is near White Sulphur Springs, a place turn-of-the-nineteenth century botanists could reach by train. Later botanists, more mobile, have also found it in other parts of West Virginia and in Maryland, Virginia, and Pennsylvania. Our second stop was along the trail over Paw Paw Tunnel Hill. A shale patch just above the upstream tunnel entrance yielded shale barren ragwort, another endemic, and again the *Paronychia*.

Along Kasecamp Road we parked and climbed a short way up a steep hill to a more typical shale barren. Under small, scattered Virginia pines few plants were growing on the shaley surface. After much searching, we finally found the inconspicuous Kates Mountain clover among other plants on the lower part of the slope, and equally inconspicuous bent milkvetch, another shale barren endemic. Both species had passed their flowering seasons, unfortunately. The clover produces yellowish-white flowers from late April to mid-May; the milkvetch white and purple flowers from late April to early May. As these dates suggest, April to mid-May, before the baking heat of summer, is the best time for a visit to a shale barren. Observe from the edges to avoid trampling rare plants.

The streams of the state forest are shallow, for the most part, and do not support good populations of game fish. However, in early spring the state stocks rainbow and brown trout (which do not occur naturally) for "put and take" fishing. This is a popular activity, but most popular at Green Ridge is hunting. Bow-hunting for deer begins in September; the rifle season runs for two or three weeks after

Thanksgiving. Turkeys are hunted in both fall and spring. Some form of game is in season from September to January, and again from mid-April to mid-May (turkeys). The forest manager advises hikers to wear bright colors during these times, or to come on Sunday, when hunting is not permitted. Check with the Maryland DNR for regulations and open seasons.

One pursuit birders can enjoy in fall without concern for hunters is hawk-watching on Town Hill, which parallels Green Ridge. Where Scenic Route 40 crosses Town Hill, there is an unobstructed view eastward and benches under a shelter where you can relax during lulls in the southward migration flight. This is considered an especially good place to see golden eagles. The Town Hill Hotel Bed and Breakfast across the highway offers accommodations. The biggest flights are those in September when conditions are right and thousands of broad-winged hawks pass by.

Walking the canal you often feel shut in by the lush foliage. From an overlook on Carroll Road, in Green Ridge State Forest, you get another perspective—a wonderful view of the river and canal, far below. It's a different world up there.

Back by Canoe or Kayak

When you walk or bike the canal, your view is often restricted by foliage, or at least bare trees, but from the surface of the river you get an entirely different perspective. The mountain ridges open up to view, as do cliffs along the river, and the changing patterns of sky and cloud. You can contemplate the human dwellings and activities along shore, and greet fellow boaters on the water.

The most popular canoe/kayak runs are from below Great Falls to Sycamore Island or Brookmont, and from Paw Paw, West Virginia, to Little Orleans or farther to Hancock. The first offers good whitewater and scenic shores. The second traverses big looping bends through the mountains, with a strong current and occasional riffles. Three miles of rapids at Harpers Ferry offer a shorter, sporting run for the more experienced boaters. The 50 miles from Spring Gap to Hancock make a very pleasant four-day, leisurely trip, with no dams, which are a hindrance and impound slow water on some sections. Boat ramps are shown on the C & O Canal NHP folder map.

Boating the river of course gets you close to aquatic wildlife. I'll describe some of the warm season species. Great blue herons lumber off, croaking. Smaller green herons yell "skeeow," and land not far away, waiting to see if you'll be a further nuisance. Wood ducks, mallards, and Canada geese are frequent sights, trailing young in the spring (geese) or summer (ducks). In recent years, black, snake-necked double-crested cormorants have become common on the upper Potomac, and some nest. Ospreys, diving from a height for fish, are most likely in spring and fall, though some, wanderers from elsewhere or possibly nesters, appear in summer. Bald eagles might be seen anywhere along the river, though most likely near the nesting sites described earlier. Ring-billed gulls are common in spring and fall, some on migration, with an occasional herring gull mixed in; the small Bonaparte's gull, with a white flash in the forewing, migrates up the river in spring. Among the smaller birds, you'll often see brown-backed, white-bellied rough-winged swallows, which nest in rock or bank crevices and holes along shore and hunt insects in languid flight out over the water. Spotted sandpipers are common in spring and late-summer to fall; a few have been found breeding along the river. They fly off on downcurved, stuttering wings and land on the water's edge, bobbing.

Drifting slowly, you might come upon a muskrat, beaver, or, with luck, an otter. As with most wildlife, these are especially active early or late in the day. Watch logs and rocks for basking turtles: the red-bellied is more likely than the smaller painted, which seems to prefer quiet, shallower water.

Among insects, dragonflies are common and mayflies may be emerging from the water, as nymphs molt to the winged form. These then molt once more, becoming adult. The males swarm, dancing in unison up and down to attract females. Living only long enough to produce eggs—a day or two—mayflies then die. Their order, thus, is named Ephemeroptera. Some 10 to 15 species live in the upper Potomac. Common species include the reddish brown March brown (*Stenema vicarium*), which emerges in April; the big, dark gray to black slate-winged drake (*Hexagenia* sp.), which hatches in late June and July; and the white miller (*Ephoron leucon*), late July to early August.

There is a great diversity of fishes below you, but of course very little of this comes to view. In spring carp noisily spawn in the shallows, their backs rising above the surface. Bass and other predatory fish chase smaller fish, sometimes causing them to leap from the water or race toward shore. Drop a line in the water and you may learn more about what's down there and where fish prefer to live. (See Overview: Fishing the Canal and River; also the checklist of fish.)

Boating or walking the river's edge in summer, one often encounters big patches of water willow in shallow water. *Photo by Connie Durnan.*

Kayaker with big dog.

Two aquatic plants are especially conspicuous. Usually by summer there are great patches of water stargrass (*Heteranthera dubia*), which has long grasslike strands and small, pale yellow flowers. Covering the surface and subsurface, it provides hiding places for fish and frustration for anglers as it snags lures. In shallow water, water willow (*Justicia americana*), with slender willowlike leaves and pale violet or white flowers, blooms from June to October.

My boating on the Potomac has been by canoe, so I'll describe a descent of the river from a canoeist's point of view. Since mileages on the river of course are not marked, I'll identify locations mostly by estimated mileages and landmarks. I started at Cumberland, putting in on the left (facing downstream) bank. This bank is now so grown up in trees and bushes that a put-in farther downstream should be sought. A convenient place to start is Spring Gap, about 11 miles downriver from Cumberland.

Residential and industrial areas greet the canal traveler for the first 8 miles below Cumberland, but on the river you see little of this—instead, wooded shores and high cliffs. About a mile above the settlement of North Branch, a low rock dam near the site of the former Pittsburgh Plate Glass Company presents a choice: run the break on the right side, which is about a Class III rapid, or carry around. About 11 miles down the narrow river from Cumberland the Spring Gap Recreation Area, on the Maryland side, offers a camping spot. This might be a wise choice, since the next park service campsite easily accessible from the river is the Potomac Forks Hiker-Biker, some 20 miles from Cumberland but 9 miles from Spring Gap. Camping on islands administered by the park service or the state of Maryland is not permitted, and private landowners may have the same policy. From Potomac Forks on, nearly all of the NPS campsites, spaced every few miles, are near the river. You do need to have a good idea of their location, because no signs announce them on the river shore. Carry at least the park service folder on the C & O Canal, whose maps show campsites.

For those first 20 miles the North Branch of the Potomac is a relatively small, intimate, and shady stream. At Potomac Forks the South Branch enters, broadening the river, and enlarging the boater's view. One sees the mountain ridges as they appear ahead: Town Hill, Sideling Hill, Tonoloway Ridge, and Cacapon Mountain.

Below Paw Paw, West Virginia, the river bends in great loops until past Little Orleans, and mountain slopes rise steeply from the shore. The current continues as it has from the start, fairly perky, with occasional riffles and low rock ledges, over which one must pass where a smooth V of water points downstream. A strong riffle runs through the ruins of Dam No. 6, just above the mouth of the Cacapon River.

Below Hancock the river leaves the mountains and traverses the broad Hagerstown Valley. The limestone bedrock of the valley outcrops along the river in mostly low bluffs, though there is a beautiful high one between Dam No. 5 and Williamsport on the West Virginia side. You must carry around Dam No. 5, on the left, Maryland side, and one-half mile below Williamsport, around the 4-foot-high Pepco plant dam, on the right. The put-in below this dam is rather tricky—down a steep bank, and you must avoid the churning water at the foot of the dam.

Two miles downriver, the 13-mile slackwater behind Dam No. 4 begins, with its attendant row of dwellings on the West Virginia side. As Edward Gertler says in *Maryland and Delaware Canoe Trails*, "these include mobile homes, old school buses, trailers, shacks, and anything else that someone thought of to keep the rain off their heads, all often crammed together like a long parking lot." Elsewhere, particularly farther downstream, one sees quite attractive homes perched high on bluffs. Along the Maryland shore, mostly park service land, there are only a few clusters of cottages.

Below both Dam No. 5 and Dam No. 4 (carried on the left, 22 miles below Dam No. 5), you are apt to see fishermen on the rocks or in anchored boats seeking channel catfish and other species. Now the water speeds up, making for a more pleasant journey. A few miles below Dam No. 4 one comes upon the Horsebacks, a staircase of tiny ledges that run parallel to the direction of the river rather than across it. During low water look for old fish trap weirs in the first 5 miles below Dam No. 4.

At the Route 34 bridge crossing the river at Shepherdstown, look for the mud nests of cliff swallows near the top of the bridge, on the downstream side. More chunky than the familiar, streamlined barn swallow, cliff swallows can be identified by their short, square tail, white forehead, and tawny rump. (See Mile 72.7 on the towpath.)

About 3 miles below the mouth of Antietam Creek and the adjacent campground is Hooks (or House) Falls. Canoeists can avoid this ledge by running down a sluice cut out of the limestone bottom along the West Virginia shore. This was dug around 1769 so boats could carry iron ore upstream to the Frederick Forge.

A kayaker runs rapids at Harpers Ferry.

Having to this point encountered little more than riffles, you finally reach the beginning of 3 miles of white water at Dam No. 3, with Harpers Ferry visible on the hill downstream on the right. The remains of this dam could be run, but the iron reinforcing rods that project upward underwater make this risky. Carry around on the left. Now it's time to thread your way through the long series of rocks and ledges known as the Needles. The water quiets as you pass high bluffs and the railroad bridge crossing to Harpers Ferry, but then, after the mouth of the Shenandoah River on the right, you encounter two more rapids, of which the second, Whitehorse Rapids, is the biggest between Cumberland and Great Falls. Beyond this, a ledge or two must be carefully negotiated, and then it's just fairly swift and riffly down to Point of Rocks. There, as at other high rock outcrops along the river, you might spot a raven soaring over the cliff on the Maryland side.

Six miles farther down you pass the Monocacy River with its long aqueduct. At the Dickerson Power Plant, if you stay close to the Maryland shore, you'll see the warm-water effluent channel, the upper part of which was modified into a practice course for the U.S. whitewater slalom team. There, rounded artificial rocks rise from the froth like high-backed turtles. (See Mile 40.6 on the towpath.)

At Whites Ferry, the Gen. Jubal Early plods back and forth, ferrying cars, and 4 1/2 miles farther down, you pass a boat ramp on the Maryland side at Edwards Ferry. Between Point of Rocks and Edwards Ferry there's a good chance of seeing a bald eagle.

The river has been pretty quiet ever since Point of Rocks, but at Dam No. 2, a mile downstream from Seneca Creek and its aqueduct, the river enters the Seneca Breaks, a mile of swift, usually shallow, rocky water. Most canoeists and kayakers prefer to cross the river above the dam and run down the skirting channel along the Virginia shore, through woods. Originally the Virginia Canal, built by George Washington's Patowmack Company to permit navigation around the Seneca rapids, it fell into disrepair by 1830 and today bears no resemblance to a canal. This can be tricky, with frequent small rapids and the possibility of a fallen tree blocking the way. Be especially alert for such an obstruction, as it can flip your boat and pin you underwater.

The Potomac downstream from Harpers Ferry has many islands, and these add interest to one's trip. The next section, down to Great Falls, has one island, Conn, of special interest from a natural history point of view. Look for great blue heron nests on the upstream half, along the left side of it facing downstream. There's an eagle's nest near the downstream end of the island (as described at Mile 14.4 on the towpath). You should view this from the concrete overlook near the Great Falls Tavern, as the nest is near a dam. Next, immediately get near the Maryland shore and land well above the dam, which is at the water intake.

A very few expert kayakers with detailed knowledge of it run Great Falls at low water levels, but normal people should end their downriver trip at Great Falls Tavern. Determined river travelers could carry around the falls along the towpath and reach the river down a trail from about Mile 14 for a run through a side channel, if water levels are high enough, into swirling waters in the deep Mather Gorge. The next river access is 1.7 miles farther down at Angler's Inn.

Many canoeists and kayakers regard the section from Great Falls to Little Falls as the Potomac's finest. Though near Washington, the deep, forested valley looks wild, and rapids at Yellow Falls and Stubblefield Falls, as well as the large standing waves at the foot of Great Falls, provide excitement. Boaters should take out at Sycamore Island or above Brookmont to avoid the low, water-intake dam (which has drowned people in the reversal at its foot) at the large pumping station on the Maryland side. Below this dam, the rocky remains of Dam No. 1 divert water into a channel on the left where many top kayakers practice on a slalom run. Only experts should consider proceeding downriver from the water-intake dam, as continuous rapids climax in the heavy, dangerous water of Little Falls, which also has drowned people.

Little Falls marks the end of the upper Potomac and the beginning of tidewater. One can explore the few river miles from here down to Key Bridge most easily from Fletcher's Boathouse, at Mile 3.2 on the towpath.

For further details on boating the upper Potomac, see Gertler (1996) or, for local, family excursions, MacKay (2008).

Overviews
Hiking and Biking the Towpath

The C & O Canal towpath offers hikers and bikers a superlative, virtually level avenue through nature and history that under normal conditions is easy going. After rain or snow, however, the surface gets sloppy and may impede travel for several days, particularly for bikers. Winter and early spring have the most "mud days." The degree of solitude varies widely with time and place. Weekends, holidays, and vacation times are busiest, especially those in the warmer months. Use is heaviest from Washington to Seneca and near Harpers Ferry. On some days bicycle traffic in the Washington-Seneca stretch becomes a real annoyance for walkers, and perhaps for bikers as well. The most remote sections are from Shepherdstown to Dam 4 and, with short local exceptions, from Hancock to North Branch. Brunswick, Williamsport, Hancock, and Cumberland are the major sources of food, other supplies, and services along the Maryland side of the Potomac.

With frequent campsites and a scarcely noticeable grade, the towpath is especially good for tenderfoot backpackers. Distance between most campgrounds is 4 to 8 miles, though separations range up to 12 miles. Portable toilets, fire grills, and water (with the exception of no water at Big Woods Hiker-Biker—water is 1/5 mile downstream; and no potable water in winter at any of the campgrounds) are provided at these sites. Hiker-biker campsites, the predominant type (there are also five drive-in campgrounds, where camping fees apply), in most cases have only one or two grills.

In my experience, the pleasure of backpacking is inversely proportional to the weight carried and the distance walked per day. If you are a beginner, 4 to 8 miles a day is plenty. Comfortable boots, a sleeping bag warm enough for the expected weather, and a waterproof shelter are essential for a successful trip. Day hikes can be started at many access points along the canal.

Photo by Connie Durnan.

Much of the camping on the canal is done by cyclists, who appreciate the rare combination of long distance, natural setting, reasonably smooth surface, and absence of motorized vehicles. Some places are bumpy with rocks or tree roots, and muddy spells can wreck a trip, but most of the time and most of the way the going is comfortable. Occasional detours because of construction, repair, or excessive roughness are a minor inconvenience and are well signed. For occasional bikers, 20 miles is a reasonable daily chunk; for aficionados, probably 40 to 60 miles. (I fall in the first category and find that a sore seat is more of a limiting factor than fatigue.)

Several publications, available at the National Park Service visitor centers at Georgetown, Great Falls Tavern, Brunswick, Williamsport, Hancock, and Cumberland, give further information for canal travelers. At the least, you should have the NPS C & O Canal folder, which has a map and describes the park and its recreational opportunities. Mike High's *The C & O Canal Companion* is an excellent mile by mile guide, with extensive notes on the history of the area. Thomas Hahn's *Towpath Guide to the Chesapeake and Ohio Canal* briefly describes hundreds of points of interest and is replete with history and natural history notes. *184 Miles of Adventure: Hiker's Guide to the C & O Canal*, prepared by the Baltimore Area Council, Boy Scouts of America, gives similar but much less detailed information. (See Further Reading for additional publications.)

Memorable Floods

Floods are a fact of life along any big river, and the Potomac is no exception. The biggest in recent years occurred in 1996. On January 6, snow started falling and didn't stop until 36 inches had accumulated. A few days later, 6 more inches fell. Unusually cold weather prevented its melting until the weather suddenly turned warm on January 18 and 2 inches of rain fell. This precipitated a major flood, made all the more destructive by ice floes swept along by the raging current.

The flood waters covered more than 80 percent of the canal, ripping out canal banks and damaging many historic structures. When they receded, a park service report said, "Large sections of the canal towpath and recreational units are covered with deep mud, silt, and debris. Downed trees are across many areas of the towpath.... Large piles of building debris and hazardous materials such as propane tanks and fuel tanks are scattered throughout the flood plain."

Many volunteers pitched in to help clean up their beloved canal, but estimates for repair ranged to $20 million or more. Then, when most of the towpath was again open for use, Hurricane Fran struck. The peak flooding, on September 8, was nearly as damaging as the January one. Repairs had to start from scratch, and it would be years before they were finished.

Yet the January 1996 flood was by no means the worst to hit the canal. It was exceeded in magnitude by the flood of June 24, 1972, and had only three-fourths the volume of the flood that struck in October 1942. It was even smaller in comparison with the deluge of 1936, the biggest Potomac flood since accurate records were kept in 1931. On March 18, 1936, the river roared through the streets of Cumberland, carrying with it telephone poles and automobiles. On March 19, the crest reached Washington, and would have poured into the Federal Triangle, in the center of the city, if it had not been stopped by a levee of sandbags hastily built across the Mall. Flood marks along the Potomac indicate that the "Johnstown Flood" of 1889 nearly equaled that of 1936. It produced such bizarre effects as fish being caught in Pennsylvania Avenue and a schooner being stranded near the Washington Monument. Other notable floods are sprinkled through the historical records back at least as far as 1733.

The Potomac goes over its banks, at least in some places, about every two years. Above Chain Bridge, near Washington, it rises out of its channel several times in a typical year. Such periodic breakouts are part of the nature of a river. Its channel is adjusted to carry normal flows but not the occasional very high flows. On the Potomac, many floods occur in late winter and spring, when snow is melting in the headwaters. If heavy rains come at this time, as they did in March 1936, the double burden is too much for the soil and river channel to handle. Other floods are caused by hurricanes. Such was the case in 1942 and 1972, and, as we saw, in September 1996. Hurricane Agnes, in 1972, was expected to continue up the coast but instead turned westward into Pennsylvania, dumping 1 to 3 inches of water on the upper Potomac basin. The soil, already saturated from an unusually wet spring, could absorb no more and the excess all went down the river valley. The geographic extent of rainfall is also important, because the watershed extends into West Virginia, Virginia, and Pennsylvania, and includes major streams such as the Shenandoah River and the South Branch of the Potomac. A downpour in one or two tributary valleys, which might cause local flooding, usually will have no big effect on the main stem, but if many or all of the tributaries become swollen, the total contribution is likely to mean a flooding Potomac.

The shape of the river's valley dictates where a flood will rise the highest. In sections where the flood plain is wide, the excess water has plenty of room to spread, and consequently does not reach very high on the valley slopes. But where the river runs between high walls and has little or no flood plain, the water has nowhere to go but up. This effect is most dramatic at Harpers Ferry and especially below Great Falls. Looking at the deep Mather Gorge below the falls, one can hardly imagine that the water could rise above it; but on several occasions it has done just that, drowning the falls and reaching to the buildings high on the Virginia shore, and to Great Falls Tavern on the Maryland side.

The 1936 flood, the largest since 1920, sweeps past Lock 6.
Courtesy of C & O Canal National Historical Park.

Floods damage the canal both by breaking its banks and by depositing silt. Some of the principal break points are above Four Locks, at Harpers Ferry, at Widewater, and above Georgetown. Silting of the canal bed, a problem that was worse than breaks in operating days, occurs mainly in the lowest sections—those that are closest to the normal level of the river.

Though floods are natural and inevitable, some steps have been taken to reduce their magnitude. After the 1936 flood, the Potomac at Cumberland was channelized in concrete to handle more water and move it rapidly by the city, and a dam was built on an upstream tributary to capture excess runoff. Reforestation of marginal farmland and regrowth of cutover forests probably have helped to reduce flood crest heights. But when the really heavy rains come or deep snow melts fast, there is nothing to do but get out of the way. As it has for millennia, the Potomac is going to flood.

Largest Floods of the Potomac River since 1920

Date	Cubic feet per second at Little Falls
March 19, 1936	484,000

October 17, 1942	447,000
June 24, 1972	359,000
April 28, 1937	347,000
January 21, 1996	347,000
November 7, 1985	317,000
September 8, 1996	314,000
May 14, 1924	295,000 (approx.)
August 20, 1955	216,000

Geology of the Potomac Valley

One of the many benefits of that marvelous nature trail, the C & O Canal towpath, is the glimpse it gives of a large segment of the earth's history, written in the rocks so abundantly exposed along its route. If you know the nature and origins of the rocks, you will understand much about the topography of the land and the land's capacity to support life. The rocks, indeed, are our foundation.

Rock formations along the canal range in age from Precambrian (1.1 billion years) to Triassic (181-230 million years). The I-68 road cut at Sideling Hill exposes a striking portion of this geologic history, a syncline of early Mississippian (about 330-345 million years) sedimentary formations. *Photo by Connie Durnan.*

Deposition, uplift, and erosion of the rocks have produced much variety in the topography of the Potomac basin. Five major physiographic provinces, each with its own subdivisions, have been recognized: the Coastal Plain, Piedmont, Blue Ridge, Valley and Ridge, and Appalachian Plateaus. The Coastal Plain, underlain by deposits of sand, clay, gravel, and shells, is level to gently rolling. The Piedmont, in its eastern section, is hilly land underlain by hard, resistant rocks; in the west are the rather level Frederick Valley of Maryland and the Leesburg Basin in Virginia, both formed by erosion of the relatively soft, underlying red sandstone, shale, and limestone. Rocks of the Blue Ridge Province, which extends from Catoctin Mountain west to South Mountain and the Blue Ridge, consist mostly of Precambrian (now called Proterozoic) granitic gneisses. The Valley and Ridge Province is a series of parallel mountain ridges separated by narrow or wide valleys eroded in limestone or shale. In the east, this province begins with the Shenandoah Valley in Virginia and the equally wide Hagerstown Valley in Maryland. Both are parts of the Great Valley that runs (geologically if not in name) from Canada to Alabama. Farther west, ridges and valleys rapidly succeed each other as far as the Allegheny Front, several miles beyond Cumberland, where the high, rolling plateau province begins. The canal cuts through the three middle provinces of this sequence—the Piedmont, Blue Ridge, and Valley and Ridge—but its essential function was to connect the coal fields of the Appalachian Plateaus with navigable tidewater in the Coastal Plain.

In places between Point of Rocks and just east of Harpers Ferry, ancient basement rocks 1.1 billion years old are exposed along the canal, but most of the rocks owe their origin and shaping to events that came later. These events, in essence, were the unimaginably long filling of a giant trough in the Iapetus Ocean, which formed when rifts separated the North American and African continental plates, and the subsequent upraising, folding, and erosion of the deposits in that trough.

Most of the rocks you see between Washington and Cumberland are sedimentary—sandstone, shale, limestone, and intergradations between these. They were formed from deposits in shallow water. How do we know? Because mud cracks, raindrop pits, cross-bedding, salt-crystal casts, and other phenomena of shallow water or muddy conditions can be seen in the rock, as well as fossils of plants and animals that lived in shallow water. Yet the sedimentary layers in parts of the Potomac area are as much as 5 1/2 miles thick! The apparent contradiction is explained in this way: the deposits accumulated in a trough-like area whose bottom was slowly sinking at about the same rate that the sediments were building up. This gigantic depression occupied the area of the present Appalachian Mountains and perhaps of the Piedmont as well. The sediments that filled it are believed to have come from an island arc to the east, roughly where the coastal plain now lies. This is deduced from the fact that sediments in the eastern part of the trough area are generally coarser-grained than those farther west; the larger grains, being heavier, are dropped first by streams flowing from a source area.

Of course, it took a very long time to accumulate 5 1/2-mile-thick deposits—all the 350 million years of the Paleozoic Era. This long period, during which climates were warm and most of the major steps of evolution occurred, ended with a crash—the slow crash of Africa against North America. Riding on giant plates of the earth's crust, these two continents came into contact along the Mid-Atlantic Ridge, creating intense pressures that wrinkled and fractured the rocks of eastern North America. The end result was high mountains where shallow seas had been. The mountains we see now are remnants, worn down, perhaps with intermediate periods of uplift, from the more majestic and rugged originals. In many places along the canal you can see folds in the rock layers formed when the earth's crust was wrinkled by that slow, immense pressure from colliding continents.

How does the Potomac River fit into all this? Some geologists think it developed, in approximately its present course, sometime after the major period of mountain-building, about 300 million years ago. Others, however, place the river's age at only 10 to 20 million years. Whatever its age, it has carved its channel in accordance with changes in the land surface. The great meanders below Paw Paw and below Williamsport must have formed when the land there was nearly level, causing the river to flow very slowly and allowing it to wander. Later, during uplift of the land or increased flow during the wet, snowy Pleistocene, when sea levels dropped, the river cut deeper, entrenching itself and leaving terraces at its earlier levels. (See Profile of the Valley Forest.) River gaps through ridges, such as the spectacular one at Harpers Ferry, are the product of simultaneous uplift of the mountains and downcutting by the stream.

The character of the rocks and the work of the river in carving a deep or shallow valley and creating flood plains have had a profound influence on life. These things shape the contours of the land and strongly influence the kinds of soil that develop, and this in turn, with climate, sets limits for the kinds of plants and animals that can live there and the types of human activity that can be carried on.

Limestone and shale, for instance, erode more rapidly than sandstone and therefore usually floor the valleys. Sandstone or its derivative, quartzite, caps most of the Appalachian ridges. The uppermost rock layer (bedrock) influences soils by the size and mineral constituents of the particles the rocks weather into. Sandstone contributes sand, whose large grains leave big air spaces between them and therefore allow water to percolate down rapidly, making the upper layers dry. Limestone, on the other hand, weathers into smaller, more closely packed particles that allow less air space and present more total surface area for soil water to cling to; limestone particles also contribute calcium, a very important mineral for plants. Thus the richest farmland along the canal is in the Frederick and Hagerstown valleys, carved in limestone. The topography created by erosion working on the rocks influences soils and the life that depends on them primarily through steepness of slope; the steeper the slope, the faster the runoff and consequent drying of the soil. So plants, whether domestic or wild, and the animals and humans that depend on them, flourish best where the rocks dictate valleys and rich, water-holding soils. The river, in building flood plains, has achieved a similar result.

Floodplain Trees

Much of the forest that grows along the canal is made up of a distinctive group of trees—species that can live with a high water table and withstand periodic flooding and ice damage, as well as being able to germinate and get started in this difficult habitat. From the river shore up to an elevation of 10 to 20 feet above the normal water level, silver maple, sycamore, green ash, boxelder, eastern cottonwood, American elm, black willow, river birch, and hackberry are the principal members of the forest. Each has a different appearance and adaptations for surviving in this rich but stressful environment.

The American sycamore is easily identified by its white bark and large, maple-like leaves. It often reaches a height of 100 feet and a diameter ranging from 3 to 10 feet. *Leaves photo by Connie Durnan.* (above and opposite)

You will see black willow, cottonwood, river birch, and sycamore most frequently at the very edge of the river or canal. These species can withstand frequent flooding, and they require mineral soil, which scouring or depositing by water provides, for germination of the seeds. The seedlings need full sunlight for survival and growth, and this, too, a riverside or island location often gives. Black willow, cottonwood, and river birch are successional trees: they colonize open ground but die out when long-lived, shade-tolerant species overtop them. (However, typical tree succession may be rare on flood plains, where floods frequently destroy trees and hold back the process.) River birch, a southeastern

tree, is notable for its shaggy, peeling, pinkish bark. Continuance of cottonwood, here at the eastern edge of its range, is helped by openings created by beaver cutting, although at the same time it is hindered by beavers, which cut the soft cottonwoods down. The white-barked sycamore can live for 250 years or more and thus remain a member of the floodplain forest even where suitable germination sites have become scarce. Old sycamores tend to become hollow, making homes for squirrels, raccoons, wood ducks, owls, woodpeckers, starlings, and a host of other animals.

Green ash and boxelder are two more successional species that may be abundant in a relatively young forest but die out if the forest matures. Green ash has finely furrowed bark and opposite leaves, each broken into 5 to 9 leaflets. Boxelder, a maple with leaflets resembling poison ivy, is a smaller tree that sometimes forms dense stands. Many of its seeds remain on the tree all winter; these seeds were a prime attraction for evening grosbeaks, striking black and yellow birds from the north, in the years when they commonly wintered this far south.

The silver maple leaf has five deeply cut, coarsely toothed lobes and the tree reaches a height of 60 to 80 feet. *Photo by Connie Durnan.*

Silver maple, probably the most abundant large tree on Potomac flood plains, grows at the water's edge and throughout the low-lying forest. It flowers from February to April and in our area drops most of its numerous, winged seeds in the last half of April. Thousands are sprouting in May, on bare, moist, water-scoured soil. But new seedlings will survive only under certain circumstances: they must have sunlight, freedom from competition with tall weeds, and time to grow large enough to withstand the next flood.

American elm is less particular about its seedbed. Although the seedlings do best on mineral soil, they can become established on moist litter, moss, or decayed logs. Elms are shade-tolerant and long-lived, too, thus allowing the species to remain indefinitely in the floodplain forest. Unfortunately, these graceful trees are disappearing here as well as on city streets, victims of Dutch elm disease. Hackberry has a similar, though less graceful, form. It can be quickly identified in any season by the warty or ridged gray bark. Many birds, such as robins, bluebirds, and wild turkeys, eat the fruits. In some places along the Potomac, beavers have cut this species to the apparent exclusion of all others.

There are several characteristics common to many floodplain trees. In addition to an ability to tolerate inundation, the seeds of many, such as the winged silver maple and the plumed sycamore, cottonwood, and black willow, float well and remain viable even after long periods in the water. Several species, among them silver maple, boxelder, and sycamore, readily sprout from the stump; this is a useful characteristic in an environment where floating logs and ice floes frequently shear off trees during high water.

Get to know these trees of the river bottom. You will meet them often along the canal.

Profile of the Valley Forest

Along much of the Potomac are level lands called flood plains and above these, in places, are terraces. These features of the landscape determined much of the canal's route, as well as the types of forest found on them. To some extent, they influence the animal life too.

Flood plains have been built by the river, and as the name implies, they are covered (to various degrees) by water during floods. Some of the material in these plains has been dropped there by water flowing over them, but most of the flood plain is built in a different way. In a broad valley a river has room to move sideways. On the outer, concave side of a bend, where the current is strongest, the water eats away the bank; and on the inner, convex side, where the current is slower, it drops sediment. Thus the bend migrates more or less sideways, building "point-bar deposits" on the inner side. When the river finally bumps up against bedrock on the side of the valley, it is forced to stop migrating in that direction and may start shifting its channel back toward the other side. The flood plain, then, is made mostly of point-bar deposits left behind by the lateral wandering of the river.

Some rivers do a lot of wandering; the Mississippi, especially in its lower, undammed section, is a classic example. But the Potomac doesn't move much. In many places trees 200 or more years old grow on its banks. The primary reason is that for most of its length the Potomac is entrenched within a narrow, steep-sided valley. Only from Whites Ferry to Seneca is there a long stretch with room for a broad flood plain.

But this entrenched condition was not always so. Far back in geologic history, the Potomac flowed at higher levels within a broader valley. At some time in that dim past the earth's crust began to rise and the river cut deeper into the rising rock, limiting the possibilities for sideways migration. Above this entrenched level were left loops where the river had once flowed and former flood plains, which are called terraces. The Potomac, for instance, once made a big bend that came near the site of Sterling, Virginia; and there are several abandoned routes of the river in the mountains above Hancock: Purslane Run, above Paw Paw, flows in one such former river channel. On the ancient flood plains, or terraces, now left high and dry, are stones that were rounded by water, presumably when that was the location of the river bed, before renewed cutting lowered the channel. Some of these terraces are as much as 2 miles from the present course of the river. Terrace gravels are especially abundant within bends of the river between Shepherdstown and Williamsport, on Praether's Neck, and between Fort Frederick and Licking Creek.

Some of the terraces and course changes of the Potomac may have occurred during the relatively recent Pleistocene, when increased precipitation caused heavier run-off and therefore increased eroding power. The terraces below Great Falls are thought to be Pleistocene in age.

The canal route in many sections takes advantage of the old river terraces. There are fairly consistent terrace systems at 20 to 40 feet, 65 to 85 feet, and 125 to 135 feet above the present river level, as well as less-distinct, higher ones; the canal particularly utilizes the 20 to 40 foot terrace and the flank of the second. In some sections where cliffs left little room, the canal was placed on man-made terraces built up at the very edge of the river.

Though the river's flood plains and terraces do not usually form neat steps, you can often discern a difference of levels, especially between the active flood plain and the first terrace. Knowing how these were created gives one an added sense of geologic history and an appreciation of the river's dynamic nature.

The shape of the land under your feet has a great deal to do with the kinds of forest and animals you see. Where the canal traverses flood plains or low terraces you see different kinds of trees than where it follows a higher terrace or the foot of a cliff; and to some extent the birds, mammals, and other animal life are different as well.

Near the river are willows, cottonwoods, sycamores, and perhaps river birches. Scattered along the shore and throughout the floodplain forest are silver maples, boxelders, green ashes, hackberries, and sometimes pin oak and other trees, with many spicebushes and paw paws, bladdernuts, and other species in the shrub layer. Wild grapes, poison-ivy, and other climbing vines cling to the trees. This is a moist, rich forest, made that way by floods, flood deposits, slow run-off, and a high water table.

Bird life, utilizing every environmental niche from the ground to the numerous tree cavities and the high treetops, is abundant. Wood ducks, barred owls, woodpeckers, and other hole-nesters are especially common here. Acadian flycatchers, American redstarts, and Kentucky warblers are among the small birds attracted to the moist, insect-laden understory. Parula and, in some sections, cerulean warblers sing from the treetops. In winter, yellow-rumped warblers, bluebirds, woodpeckers, and many other birds flock to poison-ivy berries, one of the few fruits available at this season.

Mammals are not much in evidence, but occasionally you see a gray squirrel, fox squirrel, woodchuck, or white-tailed deer, and you can bet that some of those hollow sycamores are occupied by raccoons, bats, or flying squirrels. Beavers come out at night to gnaw on preferred trees, such as willow and cottonwood.

Farther from the river shore, as the land slopes upward out of reach of all but the higher floods, trees of the uplands, such as tulip trees, oaks, and black cherry, begin to appear. On a high terrace or hillside, where floods seldom or never lap around the bases of the trees, the forest will probably be dominated by oaks: white, red, chestnut, black, and scarlet oaks are the principal species, the latter three growing on the drier slopes. Often with the oaks are various species of hickory, tulip tree (which forms nearly pure stands on some old fields), red maple, and beech. Cliffs and dry hills may be thickly covered with red cedar and pines, especially Virginia pine. Mountain laurel is a typical shrub in these upland oak forests.

Oak trees mean acorns, and acorns mean animals that feed on them. So you are more apt to see gray squirrels, blue jays, and white-breasted nuthatches on the hillsides than in the flood plain, though many species of birds and mammals, including these, range over both types of habitat. One of the most typical birds of dry slopes along the canal is the worm-eating warbler. But you are more likely to hear its thin, insect-like trill than to see its brown back and elegantly black-and-buff-striped head. On rocky hillsides, especially in the mountains, chipmunks are a common sight. Though not common, copperheads favor this habitat too.

Life in the Canal

Though most of the canal is no longer fully watered, rain, streams, and beavers keep long stretches of it pond-like or marshy. Whether you are walking past water 8 feet or 8 inches deep, there is aquatic life to be seen.

The principal deep-water sections are Georgetown to Violettes Lock (near Seneca), Big Pool and Little Pool (below Hancock), and Town Creek to Oldtown.

These are the waters that hold the larger fish, among which are carp, channel catfish, white sucker, bullhead, bluegill and pumpkinseed sunfish, pickerel, smallmouth and largemouth bass, and crappie; rainbow trout are stocked at Oldtown and Big Pool. It's not unusual to see a bright orange goldfish just below the surface—grown much larger in the canal than it had been in someone's aquarium. Providing food for some of the bigger fish are various members of the minnow family: blacknose and longnose dace, creek chub, spotfin shiner, and others. But fish are hard to see unless they're on the end of your line. More visible are the turtles that sometimes float near the surface or bask on logs, frogs that sit near the water's edge, and snakes that ripple across the surface. Binoculars will help you identify what you're seeing.

Red-bellied turtles taking the sun. They are much larger than the painted turtle, which often basks with them. *Photo by Connie Durnan.*

Shallow pools with logs and rocks often offer a better show than the deep-water stretches. If you stand or sit quietly beside one of these pools, you may see, for instance, several kinds of turtles. Painted turtles, or sliders, are common baskers on logs. With them may be red-bellied turtles, twice the size of a painted. It seems to prefer deeper water than the painted turtle, however. The little musk turtle, or stinkpot, is a common bottom feeder that seldom crawls out to bask; it can be identified by its dark, rounded shell and the two light lines on the side of its head. You may also see the ridged shell of a large snapping turtle, floating at the surface; these big-headed, fierce-looking creatures catch fish and

The northern water snake occurs in all sorts of aquatic habitats, hunting frogs, salamanders, fish, and crayfish. *Photo by Connie Durnan.*

other animals up to the size of ducks, in addition to eating plants. The frogs you are most likely to see are the large green frog and the even larger, deep-voiced bullfrog. Look among rocks or debris for a sunning water snake. These blotched, reddish-brown snakes feed mostly on aquatic life: frogs, salamanders, fish, and crayfish. If the water is shallow or clear enough, you may see a red-spotted newt. This species of salamander usually goes through a land stage, known as the red eft, before returning to the water and transforming into an adult. Muskrats are the chief aquatic mammals along the towpath; beavers and mink are sometimes seen, and otters have been reintroduced. The watcher at the canal may also see one of the numerous birds that take food from the water, such as kingfishers, herons, ducks, and a few kinds of shorebirds.

Shells of the Asiatic clam, a small, nonnative invader, litter canal and river shores.

Anchored in the bottom mud, several kinds of mussels filter food from the water. Most of the native species are scarce; only the eastern elliptio is considered secure in Maryland. The small Asiatic clam is an abundant nonnative competitor with the threatened natives. You may see rows of its empty shells along shorelines.

All the larger animals, however, form only the tip of the pyramid of life in the water. Supporting them are countless insects and other small invertebrates, including a dense soup of microscopic animals; and supporting these are myriad plants, from the microscopic phytoplankton to spadderdock and cattails. Insects include water beetles, water striders, and the larval forms of many species, such as midges, mosquitoes, mayflies, and dragonflies. Among the common aquatic plants are duckweed, whose tiny round green leaves often carpet the surface; broad-leaved arrowhead; and blue flag (an iris). In some places pondweed grows abundantly beneath the surface; and watercress, an introduced species now well-established in the wild, can be found near springs, especially in limestone country.

Since most aquatic animals are cold-blooded, activity in the canal slows way down in winter. Frogs and turtles are hibernating in the bottom mud; snakes are underground ashore; and fish reduce the tempo of their life to conserve energy. But you can still occasionally see a muskrat; mallards and black ducks drop in to feed; and kingfishers and great blue herons fish.

Spring and summer treat canal visitors to a wonderful sequence of amphibian voices. This serenade begins in late February to early March with the finger-running-over-a comb sound of the tiny chorus frog and the peeping of spring peepers. From early- to mid-March wood frogs (quacking) and pickerel frogs (snoring) tune in. Then it's American toads (long trilling) in late March to early April, and green frogs (banjo twanging) in early- to mid-April. In late April to May, cricket frogs (pebble clicking), Fowler's toads (bleating), gray treefrogs (short trilling), and bullfrogs, with their deep "jug-a-rum," join in. During summer most of the chorus fades out, but green frogs, bullfrogs, Fowler's toads, and gray treefrogs continue, their breeding seasons not yet over. Though you may never see some of these species, you can still recognize and enjoy their songs.

Fifty degrees Fahrenheit seems to be an important boundary temperature for many forms of life. It may bring out certain butterflies in winter or early spring. The tree line in Canada roughly follows the 50-degree July isotherm. In the canal, painted turtles may be basking on logs when the thermometer approaches this temperature. On one such day—a February 18—I counted 41. This may also be the level of warmth that triggers early frog calls.

Distinguished by the black patch extending backward from the eye, the small wood frog delivers a loud "quack" during its early spring breeding season in canal or woodland pools. *Photo by Connie Durnan.*

This mother wood duck with three ducklings hid behind cattails in the canal near Oldtown. One duckling feasts on duckweed. *Photo by Connie Durnan*.

With the cooling of canal waters in fall, the reptiles and amphibians again disappear. The wood ducks of summer fly south, and many plants shrivel to brown stalks. You are left with the few hardy water birds and mammals, or perhaps only a glimmering avenue of ice.

Wild Corridor—
North Meets South

Since rivers flow through the lowest land of a region, the elevational gradient up river valleys tends to be less than in the same direction on the uplands. Therefore the temperature gradient tends to be less steep as well. Along the Potomac, which rises only 600 feet between Washington and Cumberland, a climate not much cooler than that on the coastal plain extends up the valley above Washington; and in the mountains, temperatures along the river may be several degrees higher than those on ridges only a few miles away. Perhaps partly because of this climatic effect, some plants and animals of southerly distribution range up the Potomac valley farther than they do on the nearby uplands. All that is required is the presence of suitable habitat along the river and the ability of a species to reach it. Sweetgum at Big Pool is an example.

The reverse effect—southerly or downstream extension of northern or mountain species—also occurs. The species involved are usually plants; rivers carry their seeds downstream from the mountains, and if a favorable environment, such as a cool, moist ravine, is reached, the seeds may germinate and survive. It's possible, also, that some of these species are holdovers from cooler climates in the past—relict populations. Cool limestone slopes were available for wake-robin and northern white-cedar, rocky habitat at Great Falls for moss-pink. A few patches of hemlock also occur along the Potomac to the Washington area. A clump of rosebay rhododendron, another mountain species, has been reported as far downstream as Carderock, near Washington.

In many cases, the ranges of "species-pairs"—pairs of closely related species—do not overlap much. Competition for the same kind of food and living space, plus adaptation to different climates, keeps them separated. The overlap between the northern black-capped chickadee and the southern Carolina chickadee is only about 70 miles along the river; for the northern smooth green snake and southern rough green snake it is about 30 miles. Compared with the total range of each species, these distances are small. On the uplands, where climatic gradients are steeper, the overlaps might be even less.

As you walk along the towpath, then, it is interesting to watch for the stragglers from both north and south—followers of this wild corridor.

Four Seasons

The canal visitor is fortunate in having not only many sections to choose from, but four distinct seasons as well, each with its spectacular and subtle shows. With the advancing and retreating warmth, life in its complexity flourishes and fades.

Spring wildflowers. *Photos by Connie Durnan.*

Spring beauty

Yellow trout-lily

White trout-lily

Spring travels fairly rapidly up the valley; Cumberland is not far behind Washington for any given natural event. Wildflowers are perhaps the feature spring attraction. Although something can be found blooming anytime from February to November, the most popular climax comes in April and May, with massed displays of certain species. In early April spring beauties carpet the lowland woods. In mid-April Dutchman's breeches, squirrel-corn, and yellow trout-lily capture the attention, to be followed in late April by huge patches of Virginia bluebells. In early May the bluebells are rivaled by blue phlox and golden ragwort, which then fade out as June approaches. These wildflowers can be seen in almost any rich floodplain woods along the canal; some grow on hillsides as well.

The spring wildflowers are adapted to take advantage of the sun's energy before tree leaves open and intercept much of it. Similarly, bird migrations are synchronized in large part with the emergence of insects and other animal food. Though some robins winter at this latitude, I usually expect the first flock of migrating robins around George Washington's Birthday; though at that time still dependent on berries, they may be able to find earthworms on warm, wet days. March is the prime waterfowl month; look for ducks, geese, and swans on the impounded water above dams and at the Marshall Dierssen and McKee-Beshers wildlife areas. Louisiana waterthrushes and blue-gray gnatcatchers at the beginning of the month usher in the landbird migrations of April. All through this month, squeaking flocks of blackbirds throng the canal, with congregations of goldfinches and sometimes purple finches. The spring migration peaks in late April and the first three weeks of May, as the many colorful warblers and the more drab flycatchers, vireos, and thrushes pass through. Warm south winds after cold, stormy weather can produce spectacular waves of these small migrants (though the waves of tropical migrants have diminished in recent years). The canal is one of the best places in the Potomac region to see such shows; perhaps the earlier leafing flood-plain trees have more insects than the laggard oaks of the uplands.

Meanwhile, the warming earth and water have stirred hibernating reptiles, amphibians, mammals, and insects, and certain fish have been stimulated to migrate and spawn. Swarms of midges recently transformed from aquatic pupae begin appearing in early spring, to be followed by mosquitoes, mayflies, and other insects that spend the winter as eggs or larvae underwater. Tiny chorus frogs start the spring amphibian concert with high-pitched "crrrrricking" in late February; big bullfrogs end it with bass notes from May into summer. (See Overview: Life in the Canal for further details on frogs.) Salamanders, too, begin breeding very early in spring; the Jefferson and spotted salamanders emerge with the first warm rains to lay eggs in woodland and canal pools. Most of the other species breed sometime between April and summer, although a few wait until autumn. Few mammals in the Potomac area sleep the winter away. Of these, chipmunks and woodchucks are the first to arise, in February or March. Hibernating bats, such as the little brown bat and eastern pipistrelle, are a-wing by March or April. They join more migratory species, such as silver-haired, red, and hoary bats, that have returned from the southern states. In the water migratory fish respond to slowly rising temperatures; white sucker runs can be seen in small tributary streams in March and April, and herring runs begin reaching Rock Creek and Little Falls, on the Potomac, in late March. Brushfoots, such as the eastern comma and mourning cloak, which hibernate, are among the earliest butterflies to emerge.

Dutchman's breeches

Bloodroot

May apple

Pale violet

Solomon's seal

Blue phlox and golden ragwort

Summer, which may be considered to begin with the end of tree leafing in late May, is hot and humid along the Potomac. These conditions, along with moistness and flood-given nutrients in the soil, produce an almost tropical luxuriance of plant growth. Much of the wildflower blooming shifts largely to open areas, where sunlight is abundant; daisies, asters, and other members of the composite family are the principal species. Joe-Pye weed, green-headed coneflower, and pale and spotted jewelweed are among those that linger into early fall. Swallowtails and many other kinds of butterflies nectar on the flowering plants.

Mammals may be difficult to see at this season, but aquatic life is not. Many birds can be watched as they hunt food for their young. Wood ducks are common nesters along the river. Big, flashy, black and white pileated woodpeckers—the model for Woody Woodpecker—are often seen or heard. Cardinals and many other small birds forage in the undergrowth, and with luck you may spot the brilliant yellow-orange prothonotary warbler, a bird of southern rivers and swamps that nests in tree cavities by the water's edge.

In summer the river takes on a different character, too. Dropping water levels reveal many rocks, and sections that in spring may have been full and swift become gentle riffles. Colonial (and perhaps Indian) fish traps, recognized by the V-shaped arrangement of rocks, now become visible. On the muddy shores and in shallow water, tree seedlings and aquatic plants shoot up. Massive beds of grasslike water stargrass appear. Summer along the river and canal is indeed a pleasant time of indolence and abundance.

Summer Wildflowers

Pale touch-me-not. *Photo by Connie Durnan.*

Spotted touch-me-not. *Photo by Connie Durnan.*

Common milkweed. *Photo by Connie Durnan.*

Cardinal-flower. *Photo by Connie Durnan.*

Common elderberry

Wild hydrangea. *Photo by Connie Durnan.*

Indian-pipe. *Photo by Connie Durnan.*

Joe-Pye-Weed. *Photo by Connie Durnan.*

Just as spring moves up the valley, fall moves down it, though at a more leisurely pace. As early as August, black gums and Virginia creepers start turning red in the mountains. Mountainside colors usually peak in mid-October, but in the valley the climax comes in late October. Many of the flood-plain trees, such as sycamore, silver maple, and boxelder, are not showy in fall; better color is provided by the oaks, hickories, red and sugar maples, and tulip trees on the flanking hills, which break out in shades of yellow, orange, purple, bronze, and red.

Fall bird migrations do not rival those of spring in concentration of birds, and many species have duller plumages, but the total number of birds is swelled by young of the year, and the migrations stretch out over a longer period. Thus you can see migrating warblers from August to October, and shorebirds (in the few suitable spots, such as turf farms) from July to October. Special fall sights for birdwatchers are the hawk flights along mountain ridges and the occasional appearances of golden plovers and buff-breasted sandpipers on turf farms, several of which exist between Seneca and Whites Ferry. Waterfowl bring up the rear in October and November.

Less noticeable but equally interesting are the migrations of monarch butterflies, bats, and eels. The butterflies straggle southward from late summer to October, headed toward the Gulf states and, especially, central Mexico; subsequent generations return in spring. Since they usually travel at night, migrating bats are seldom seen; and unlike night-flying birds, they emit no sound we can hear. Still, I find it exciting to think that these strange little mammals, too, are passing overhead. Perhaps most unusual are the travels of eels. In the fall, fully grown adults migrate down the Potomac and many other rivers toward their spawning ground in the ocean near Bermuda, more than 1,000 miles away. Here they will end their lives. A year and a half later, their young will somehow find their way to the rivers, where they in turn will grow up and repeat the cycle.

Fall at Lock 7. *Photo by Connie Durnan*

Winter at Lock 7. *Photo by Connie Durnan.*

November's frost ends most insect activity and sends the last cold-blooded animals into hibernation. We are faced with the starkness and simplicity of winter. In January, average minimum daily temperatures along the canal range from 24 to 28 degrees Fahrenheit and maximums from 38 to 44, so usually it is not particularly cold. Though the canal may intermittently freeze over, ice seldom forms clear across the river, and snow usually lasts only a few days. This is a good season for hikes. You feel like moving along in the brisk air and it is easier to see things—the contour of the land, geological formations, and wildlife.

The Potomac valley holds a surprising amount of wildlife in winter. Many birds stay all year or stop for the winter, attracted by thick cover and good seed crops. Along the canal a berry-laden poison-ivy vine winding up a tree may be alive with feeding robins, bluebirds, yellow-rumped warblers, cedar waxwings, woodpeckers, and other birds. Sparrows especially like the weedy fields; the Piedmont section of the valley has become a favored wintering ground for white-crowned sparrows from the northwest, along with several more common species. In past years evening grosbeaks sometimes came in numbers from the north, and perhaps they will again, feeding on the abundant seeds of boxelders, ash, and tulip trees. Many woodpeckers and other forest birds hunt insect larvae in bark and dead wood. Bird-eating hawks—Cooper's, sharp-shinned, and (rarely) goshawks—settle in for the winter, hunting the woods and edges, and other hawks frequent the open fields. On the river waterfowl, especially Canada geese, common mergansers, goldeneyes, buffleheads, mallards, and black ducks, dive for fish and mussels or eat plants. The Washington, D.C. Christmas Bird Count illustrates the diversity here; in most years, over 50 species are found between Cabin John and Key Bridge. The District of Columbia Audubon Society conducts annual mid-winter bird counts along the entire C & O Canal; you can study the results on their web sites.

Along with the birds in the Potomac valley, you can see mammals up to the size of deer, now more visible among the bare trees. Tracks in snow tell you about the ones you didn't see.

By February, signs of spring appear again; skunk cabbage pushes up in wet forest and red maple begins to bloom. You have your chance to renew old natural acquaintances and make new ones as another yearly round begins.

Indian Life in the Valley

Locked in the cocoon of our own civilization, we tend to forget the long human involvement with the land that preceded our conquest of it. In North America, this involvement began sometime during the last period of glaciation, when lower sea levels exposed a land bridge, allowing hunters to cross from Siberia into the New World (the majority belief of scientists). By 9000 BCE (before the common era) or perhaps even earlier, humans had reached the Potomac valley. Their story after that time was of a slow evolution from nomadic hunting and gathering to a settled agricultural life on the river's flood plain, as the climate changed and they discovered new ways to do things. We decipher this history from the tools, bones, and other traces they left behind.

A few fluted spear points, found on the hills at Seneca and Point of Rocks, are all we have from the Paleo-Indians who hunted along the main stem of the Potomac some 11,000 years ago; but many more of their points and flakes have been found near Front Royal, on the Shenandoah River. With ice sheets still covering most of Canada, the climate was cool and dry. Spruce forests and grasslands apparently covered much of the basin, and hunters stalked the big animals that grazed here, most likely elk, caribou, and deer, although mastodons, camels, horses, and bison also lived in this region.

As the glaciers retreated, the climate warmed. Oaks, chestnuts, and other deciduous trees began to replace conifers and grassland, and many of the Pleistocene animals died out, leaving deer, bear, and other species of the present. From 8000 to 1000 BCE—the Archaic Period—valley inhabitants increasingly turned to plant foods, such as chestnuts and berries, though hunting, particularly for deer, remained important. They learned, too, to exploit the hordes of suckers that made spawning runs in early spring and the huge sturgeons that spawned later. In spring and fall, skillful spear throwers could have brought down waterfowl at the river's edge.

About 3,000 years ago, life along the Potomac apparently became more sedentary. Bowls, made of soapstone, appear for the first time. (A large soapstone quarry existed in Rock Creek Park and a smaller one at Western Avenue and River Road, in Washington.) These heavy bowls probably were used for preparing and storing food. By this time, too, the valley Indians may have been planting wild food plants, such as goosefoot, at their settlements, though such incipient horticulture must have remained quite secondary to hunting and gathering.

In the eastern United States, Indian cultures from 1000 BCE to 1600 CE (common era) are termed Woodland. They are marked by the appearance of pottery and, most importantly, after 1 to 200 CE, by the more settled life that goes with agriculture. Before farming became dominant, there was a period of increased reliance on fish and shellfish. Judging from the numerous campsites, many groups converged on the Little Falls area in spring, when immense numbers of sturgeon, shad, and several other species were going upriver to spawn. Here the fish were concentrated by the narrow channel and slowed by heavy rapids. With hook, net, and spear, the fishermen of that time undoubtedly lined the rocky shores in April much as anglers do today. Besides fish, the river also yielded mussels and snails, which were primarily summer additions to the diet.

The several centuries before and after the birth of Christ saw the development of extensive communication networks in the Northeast. Rhyolite from Catoctin Mountain found its way far from the Potomac piedmont. Likewise, elements of the remarkable Adena culture of Ohio entered the Potomac area; burial in mounds, for instance, was adopted in the upper parts of the basin.

By what route corn agriculture reached the Potomac is not known, but the direction was generally from west to east. First domesticated in Mexico about 5,000 years ago, corn spread very slowly north and east as its cultivation was learned and strains were developed to withstand the colder climates. By 80 BCE it had reached the Midwest, and by 900 CE, if not earlier, it was being grown along the Potomac. By this time corn—along with beans, squash, and sunflowers—was the mainstay of the valley's peoples. In semi-permanent villages of 75 to 250 people, they grew it year after year on the rich flood-plain soils.

Hunting and fishing became supplementary to the agricultural harvest. Bones excavated at the Shepherd site near Seneca indicate the diversity of animals that were still sought for food and clothing: deer (most important), woodrats, squirrels, rabbits, beaver, skunk, raccoon, fox, mink, dog, bobcat, black bear, elk, turkey, duck, box tortoise, snapping turtle, painted turtle, sturgeon, sucker, freshwater mussels, and river snails. With a dependable agricultural base and an abundance of wild plants and game, the Potomac Indians of 1000 to 1500 CE seem to have reached a pinnacle of comfort.

Then came trouble. Archeological diggings at the latest Woodland sites revealed the traces of stockaded villages and occasionally an arrow point imbedded in a skeleton. What caused the conflict between tribes we do not know; perhaps it was population pressure or competition for the European fur trade. Whatever the reason, the fighting left the Potomac piedmont almost uninhabited. By the time colonial settlers pushed above tidewater, a few Piscataways were all that remained of the once-dominant tribe in Maryland. These drifted westward, and after 1700 very few Indians remained in the Potomac valley. Their cornfields, game, fish, and perhaps fish traps were taken over by white farmers, who started out using the land much as the Native Americans had before them. The Natives had pointed the way.

People, Forests, and Wildlife

Wildlife of the Potomac valley, both on land and in the water, has been profoundly affected by humans. Many of the changes are due to clearing and subsequent regrowth of the forests. Others are more direct, such as the introduction of new species or losses due to hunting. The story is heartening, disheartening, and always interesting.

A pamphlet titled "A Relation of Maryland," published in London in 1635, painted the pre-settlement wildlife scene: "In the upper parts of the countrie there are buffaloes, elkes, lions [mountain lion], bears, wolves. And deare there are in great store, in all places that are not much frequented, as also beavers, foxes, otters and many other sorts of beastes. Of birds, there is the eagle, …falcon [probably the peregrine]…; also wild turkeys in great abundance, whereof many weigh fifty pounds and upwards...." Meshach Browning, a famous hunter who roamed western Maryland in the late eighteenth and early nineteenth centuries, reputedly found timber rattlesnakes so thick in some areas that he had to wrap his legs with grasses for protection.

In subsequent years, bison, elk, mountain lions, wolves, and beavers were killed off. Deer, bear, otter, wild turkey, and rattlesnake were greatly reduced. More recently, eagles and peregrines disappeared as breeding species in the upper Potomac region. Though hunting and trapping were the principal immediate causes of most of these losses, reduction of the forests and, later, chemical contamination played an important part. These affected many other less conspicuous species as well.

Clearing of upper Potomac valley land for farms began early in the eighteenth century. By 1733, settlement had begun in the Frederick Valley east of South Mountain and in the Hagerstown Valley to the west, mostly by Germans moving south from Pennsylvania. Indian harassment and the French and Indian Wars of 1754 to 1763 halted westward progress for a time, but in the last decades of the century all the valleys to Cumberland and beyond were occupied. After the more level land along the Potomac River and in the intermountain valleys had been cleared, new arrivals tried the adjoining basal slopes and tops of the ridges.

Forest lands were diminished for other purposes, too. Many mountainsides were clear-cut to make charcoal for the iron furnaces that operated from the late 1700s until the end of the nineteenth century; Catoctin and Antietam creeks were two of the principal locations for these furnaces. Trees were also cut to make mine props, railroad ties, and structures along the canal. And from the earliest days of settlement, the best lumber trees, such as white pine, were taken for local building needs. By the end of the nineteenth century, forest clearing had reached its peak, and most of the woodlands that remained were scrubby second or third growth that was frequently ravaged by fire.

All this tree-cutting drastically reduced the habitat for such forest animals as bears, squirrels, wild turkeys, mountain lions, wolves, and rattlesnakes. But it opened new territory for grassland and forest-edge species. Woodchucks, meadow voles, and other small rodents increased. Foxes, large reptiles such as black snakes, red-tailed hawks, and other mouse-eaters no doubt benefited in turn. Bobwhites became numerous, and many birds of the Midwestern prairies, such as meadowlarks, horned larks, and vesper and grasshopper sparrows, appeared as these species extended their ranges eastward into the newly opened lands.

Early in the twentieth century the tide of clearance turned. Marginal farms in the mountains were abandoned, cutting for charcoal ceased, and people began to appreciate the value of forests for erosion control and recreation. Some of the open country grew back to forest, other areas became public land, and much scrubby woodland was given a chance to mature.

Again, wildlife was affected. Field animals declined; now, for instance, it is difficult to find a grasshopper sparrow anywhere along the canal. At the same time, forest animals increased. With the help of introductions by humans, turkeys spread and became more common, now even scratching around the outskirts of Washington. Under strict hunting regulations and with new browse growing on old fields, deer came back strongly. Similar human help, along with forest regrowth, enabled beavers to recapture territory they had lost a century earlier. The beautiful, many-hued wood duck, once hunted to the vanishing point, now is abundant along the river and its larger tributaries, thanks to a period of complete protection.

As wildlife benefited, so did the land. Erosion was slowed, and flooding diminished as the new vegetation and humus absorbed more water. In much of the Potomac valley, forest regrowth edged out agriculture. More recently, with a negative effect on wildlife, residential development is reversing the reforestation trend. Over the past 20 years or so, agricultural land uses decreased by about 350,000 acres, and urban land uses increased by about 300,000 acres, in the entire Potomac River watershed. There has been a net loss of forests. Increases of paved surfaces and houses now contribute to flooding and water pollution.

What further wildlife changes can we expect? Along the canal, field species will probably continue to decline with the shrinkage of their habitat. Among the departed, wolves and elk are not likely to be brought back, and bison definitely not. Eagles and peregrine falcons have benefited from the banning of certain pesticides. As the forest matures and perhaps spreads, two large animals are also given better odds. Bears have become a regular sight in the mountain sections of Maryland; and mountain lions, perhaps both released pets and wild animals, are occasionally reported near the canal. Coyotes have entered the region from the north and west. Forest wilderness and the wildlife that goes with it will depend, as always, on the needs and attitudes of people.

Fishing the Canal and River

The Potomac River and parts of the canal have a varied assortment of game fish, both native and introduced. Among the introduced species are smallmouth and largemouth bass, bluegill, blue catfish, and rock bass. Northern pike and muskellunge have been tried in the upper sections, but with poor results. The hybrid between these two—the "tiger muskie"—stocked annually, has done better. Two thousand to four thousand, bred at a Pennsylvania facility, are released each fall in the upper Potomac by the Maryland DNR. One lucky angler caught a tiger muskie that weighed 28 pounds and measured 45 inches. Brown and rainbow trout are regularly stocked in some of the mountain tributaries and in the canal at Oldtown, rainbows in Big Pool. Among the natives are black and white crappies, chain pickerel, yellow perch, pumpkinseed, white catfish, channel catfish, and American eel. Brook trout, native to a couple of headwater streams, have been introduced to other cool tributaries.

Smallmouth bass is the premier game fish for most Potomac anglers. They can be caught throughout the warmer months, but September and early October are considered best. Since aquatic insects, the chief food of bass, flourish best in riffles and rapids, bass populations are highest in such areas, particularly those between Hancock and the Monocacy River.

Fisherman at Dam 4. *Photo by Connie Durnan.*

The fishing changes from one part of the river to another. From Spring Gap down to Paw Paw, channel cats in deep eddies probably offer the best sport. Bass fishing picks up below Paw Paw, and it was good enough below Little Orleans to attract presidents Harrison and Hoover, among other notables. From June to September, good bass fishing and freedom from mobs of motorboats can be found by floating the river from below Dam 4 to Taylors Landing. (If you want peaceful fishing, it's best to avoid the slow waters immediately above dams, where power boats and personal watercraft are apt to be running around.) A launching ramp at the Shepherdstown bridge allows access to deep-water bass fishing there and to the Horseback riffles above the bridge. The fast water just below Dam 3, at Harpers Ferry, is good for catfish and bass, and near Goodhearts Lock (No. 34) a deep channel also offers good crappie fishing in spring and fall. The stretch from Knoxville to Brunswick is probably the most popular bass area on the river. At Point of Rocks Bridge, farther down, fishing is good for catfish and carp as well as bass. The mouth of the Monocacy is noted for carp and catfish. Whites Ferry is good for crappie in spring and fall and sometimes in winter, since the water is warmed by effluent from the PEPCO plant at Dickerson. Carp, catfish, and a few bass are also taken in winter below the plant. The rapids of the Seneca Breaks, once excellent for bass fishing, are now good but dropping in favor. Overfishing and pollution seem to have hurt the sport here. At Chain Bridge, below Little Falls, hickory shad and herring swarm by the thousands in spring, and other species can be caught through the summer and fall; the proprietor at Fletcher's Boat House can give you details. These, then, are a few suggestions. But don't let them deter you from exploring other parts of the river; any spot has something to offer.

The canal is more a place for contemplation than for exciting fishing, but it does have fish. Among these are blue and channel catfish, carp, various species of sunfish, crappie, chain pickerel, and a few bass. The main watered sections are: Georgetown to Violettes Lock, Big Pool and Little Pool, and Town Creek to Oldtown. Big and Little pools have the most variety, including white and yellow perch and crappie along with the more ubiquitous species. Big Pool and the canal at Oldtown are stocked with trout in early spring.

Fishing in the canal and river comes under Maryland state regulations. A license from the state is required for fishing in the canal and in the river above Little Falls (the head of tidewater). The Sport Fishing Guide, given when you buy your license, covers all Maryland fishing regulations.

Although the Potomac is much cleaner than it was in the 1960s, there are still too many pollutants washing in. There have been massive fish kills in two Potomac tributaries—the Shenandoah and the South Branch—since 2000. Another disturbing phenomenon is the discovery of "intersex fish"—males with eggs and females with male characteristics. The specific causes of both problems are not yet known, but are believed to be at least partly attributable to pollutants. Fish advisories for the upper Potomac, as of May 2007, include no total restriction of any species but do recommend maximum numbers of meals per year for several species. PCBs and methylmercury in fish are the principal concerns. See the Maryland Department of Environment website, www.mde.state.md.us, for details.

Managing the Park

The C & O Canal National Historical Park is an interesting but sometimes difficult management challenge. One hundred eighty-four and one-half miles long and less than half a mile wide in most places, with numerous access points, it is easy to reach from the many settlements along it but for the same reason is vulnerable to impacts from outside and misuse within. The park service staff—administrators, rangers, interpreters, resource managers, and maintenance people—must ensure visitor safety, interpret the park to the public, enforce laws and regulations, protect resources, and maintain structures, the towpath, trails, and other facilities. Mostly what we users of the canal see of all this are activities and programs at visitor centers, maintenance workers repairing things, and an occasional ranger patrolling the towpath. But much more is going on.

Consider floods: The park service has a detailed Flood Response Plan. There are eight gauging stations on the Potomac between Cumberland and Little Falls. For each there is a list of actions to be taken in that area prior to a predicted flood crest, at specified water levels. These include patrolling the towpath and campsites to evacuate people; closure of access points; removal of portable toilets, trash cans, picnic tables, and movable park service equipment; and closure of feeder locks to prevent river water from going into the canal. The many other directions get quite specific, such as filling sand bags at certain flood levels to protect Great Falls Tavern and opening doors to lockhouses at locks 68 and 70 to limit flood water damage.

And poaching: Not just deer get poached. The long list includes turtles and salamanders for the pet trade, rattlesnakes, medicinal plants like ginseng and goldenseal, orchids, ferns, and morel mushrooms. Law enforcement rangers try to prevent this, but the task is daunting, given the length of the slender park and the small number of rangers.

I asked a natural resource manager—Dianne Ingram—what the main natural resource issues were. Besides poaching, she mentioned exotic plants, deer impact, boundary issues, recreational impact, hydropower relicensing of dams 4 and 5, and rare species.

Members of the Youth Conservation Corps pull up garlic mustard, a nonnative invasive plant that carpets flood plains in spring. *Courtesy of C & O Canal National Historical Park.*

Many exotic (non-native) plants are a threat because of their ability to spread rapidly and displace or disrupt native plant and animal communities. The park service attempts to eliminate exotics where they are invading "significant natural areas"—places with rare plants or significant animals. More than forty such areas have been designated in the park. These areas are examined for exotic invaders, and teams from the NPS National Capital Region and volunteers such as the Youth Conservation Corps come in to remove them. They work in the Great Falls to Chain Bridge area and have worked down from Cumberland and along certain tributaries, focusing partly on Japanese knotweed. Major offenders are garlic mustard, tree of heaven, Japanese honeysuckle, porcelainberry, Japanese stilt grass, lesser celandine, English ivy, gill-over-the ground, periwinkle, and princess tree.

Deer thrive in the mixture of woods and fields along the canal. Because of a lack of predators, an abundance of nearby farm crops, and other factors, deer have achieved high populations. Browse lines can be seen along the edges of many wooded areas. Deer are changing the forest composition by what they eat or don't eat. They like many wildflowers, including rare ones. Nodding pogonia, an orchid officially listed as extirpated from Maryland, was found in the Gold Mine Tract at Great Falls in 1998. Twenty-seven plants were counted. Two days later, none could be found, probably because of deer grazing. "Deer are an overwhelming issue for us," Dianne said. "It's hard to document, and harder to do something about." Most reduction methods encounter public opposition, and the long, thin configuration of the park makes reoccupation by deer easy if they are reduced within the park.

Any national park is difficult to protect from outside influences, and one with the long boundary of the C & O Canal is especially vulnerable. Adjacent development, in particular, causes watershed problems. The park service has no control over water coming into the park from upstream, and development there has increased sedimentation and flooding. Perhaps the most dramatic example of this was the torrent that came through the parking lot at Glen Echo on May 5, 1989. The culvert under the lot was unable to take all the water, which rose and swept nine cars down to the Potomac River. The only solution was to remove part of the parking lot and restore the original stream declivity.

Most recreational users of canal lands are not aware of the impact they can have—on plants particularly. They may hike off trails through important plant sites, and some rock-climbing routes in the Potomac Gorge go through locations of rare plants. This, too, is difficult to handle. Marking all sites of rare plants and warning people to stay away from them would be very time-consuming and expensive, and would invite poaching. It's best not to announce the location of rare things.

The relicensing of dams 4 and 5 deals with public agencies and a corporation, rather than the public or communities. The National Park Service owns these dams and is required to relicense use of them every 30 years for hydroelectric power generation (the licenses come from the Federal Energy Regulatory

Commission). The licenses were due to expire in 2002. Involved parties, besides the NPS, were Allegheny Energy, which operates the power-producing dams; the Maryland and West Virginia natural resource departments, which are concerned with recreational use and natural resources of the river; and the U.S. Fish and Wildlife Service, which is concerned with the dams' blockage of fish and eel movements. It took three years to decide who should do what: Allegheny Energy funded studies of the dams' impact on fish movements and of recreational use of slackwater areas, and also paid for interpretive exhibits about hydropower. The company was relicensed in 2004. In 2006, the USFWS and NPS were engaged in the design and installation of eelway passages over the dams.

The canal's natural resource managers must also know what rare, threatened, or endangered species exist in the park in order to take measures to protect them. Since many such species are not conspicuous and by definition are scarce, it takes expert study to document them. In recent years surveys have been made of plants, butterflies, and amphibians. As of 1996, 1577 species of vascular plants, 79 butterflies, 64 fishes, 36 reptiles, 26 amphibians, 266 birds, and 47 mammals had been recorded in the park. (See Appendix at the end of this book.) Of these, just one, the plant Harperella, is listed as Federally endangered, but 106, mostly plants, are state-listed as threatened or endangered in Maryland.

Since the park is difficult to patrol and it is even harder to monitor its conditions, volunteers have taken on some of the burden. For instance, certain members of the C & O Canal Association, called Level Walkers after people who conducted regular inspections during canal operating days, continue this useful function. They look not only for problems with cultural resources like locks, lockhouses, aqueducts, and the canal itself, but also note the condition or presence of important natural resources. Each periodically walks their assigned few miles of the towpath and reports findings. I did this myself for a few years and I commend this good work to others.

Further Reading

Baltimore Area Council, Boy Scouts of America. *184 Miles of Adventure: Hiker's Guide to the C & O Canal*. 1970.

Brezinsky, David. *Geology of the Sideling Hill Roadcut*. Compiled by the Maryland Geological Survey, 2300 St. Paul Street, Baltimore, Maryland 21218, 1994.

Brown, Russell G. and Melvin L. Brown. *Woody Plants of Maryland*. Pikesville, Maryland: Port City Press, 1972.

Davies, William E. *The Geology and Engineering Structures of the Chesapeake and Ohio Canal*. Glen Echo, Maryland: C & O Canal.Association, 1999.

Fleming, Cristol, Marion B. Lobstein, and Barbara Tufty. *Finding Wildflowers in the Washington-Baltimore Area*. Baltimore: Johns Hopkins University Press, 1995.

Gertler, Edward. *Maryland and Delaware Canoe Trails*. Silver Spring, Maryland: Seneca Press, 1996.

Gutheim, Frederick. *The Potomac*. New York: Rinehart & Co., 1949.

Hahn, Thomas F. *Towpath Guide to the Chesapeake and Ohio Canal*. Harpers Ferry, West Virginia: Harpers Ferry Historical Association, 1997.

High, Mike. *The C & O Canal Companion*. Baltimore: The Johns Hopkins University Press, 2000.

Hyde, Arnout Jr. and Ken Sullivan. *The Potomac: A Nation's River*. New York: Grammercy Books, 1994.

Levi, Herbert W. and Lorna R. Levi. *Spiders and Their Kin*. New York: St. Martin's Press, 2002.

MacKay, Bryan. *Hiking, Cycling & Canoeing in Maryland: A Family Guide*. Baltimore: The Johns Hopkins University Press, 2008.

National Park Service. *Chesapeake and Ohio Canal: A Guide to Chesapeake and Ohio Canal National Historical Park, Maryland, District of Columbia, and West Virginia*. Washington, D.C.: U.S. Government Printing Office, 1991.

Nikula, Blair and Jackie Sones. *Beginner's Guide to Dragonflies and Damselflies*. New York: Little, Brown and Co., 2002.

Paradiso, John. *Mammals of Maryland*. Bureau of Sport Fisheries and Wildlife, North American Fauna No. 66. Washington, D.C.: U.S. Government Printing Office, 1969.

Potomac Appalachian Trail Club. *Appalachian Trail Guide to Maryland and Northern Virginia, with Side Trails*. Vienna, Virginia: Potomac Appalachian Trail Club, 2000.

Reed, John C., Robert S. Sigafoos, and George W. Fisher. *The River and the Rocks: The Geologic Story of Great Falls and the Potomac River Gorge*. U.S. Geological Survey Bulletin 1471. Washington, D.C.: U.S. Government Printing Office, 1980.

Robbins, Chandler S. and Eirik A. T. Blom. *Atlas of the Breeding Birds of Maryland and the District of Columbia*. Pittsburgh: University of Pittsburgh Press, 1996.

Sabatke, Mark D. *Discovering the C & O Canal and adjacent Potomac River*. Rockville, Maryland: Schreiber Publishing, 2003.

Sanderlin, Walter S. *The Great National Project: A History of the Chesapeake and Ohio Canal*. Baltimore: The Johns Hopkins University Press, 1946.

Schmidt, Martin F., Jr. *Maryland's Geology*. Centreville, Maryland: Tidewater Publishers, 1993.

Southworth, C. Scott et. al. *Geology of the Chesapeake and Ohio Canal National Historical Park and Potomac River Corridor, District of Columbia, Maryland, West Virginia, and Virginia*. Reston, Virginia: U.S. Geological Survey, c. 2005.

Stanton, Richard L. *Potomac Journey: Fairfax Stone to Tidewater*. Washington, D.C.: Smithsonian Institution Press, 1993.

Stewart, Robert E. and Chandler S. Robbins. *Birds of Maryland and the District of Columbia*. Bureau of Sport Fisheries and Wildlife, North American Fauna No. 62. Washington, D.C.: U.S. Government Printing Office, 1958.

Wennerstrom, Jack. *Leaning Sycamores: Natural Worlds of the Upper Potomac*. Baltimore: The Johns Hopkins University Press, 1996.

Wilds, Claudia. *Finding Birds in the National Capital Area*. Washington, D.C.: Smithsonian Institution Press, 1992.

Appendix

Nonwoody Plants Mentioned in the Text

(Most scientific names follow M.L. Fernald, *Gray's Manual of Botany*, 1950)

Common Name	Scientific Name
Alexanders, Golden	*Zizia aurea*
Alexanders, Heart-leaved	*Z. aptera*
Alumroot	*Heuchera americana*
Aster	*Aster* spp.
Bloodleaf	*Iresine rhizomatosa*
Bloodroot	*Sanguinaria canadensis*
Blue Cohosh	*Caulophyllum thalictroides*
Blue Flag	*Iris versicolor*
Bluestem, Big	*Andropogon gerardii*
Bluestem, Little	*Schizachyrium scoparium*
Broad-leaved Arrowhead	*Sagittaria latifolia*
Buttonweed	*Diodia teres*
Carpetweed	*Mollugo verticillata*
Cinquefoil	*Potentilla canadensis*
Climbing Dogbane	*Trachyleospermum difforme*
Columbine	*Aquilegia canadensis*
Common Cattail	*Typha latifolia*
Coville's Phacelia	*Phacelia coville*
Cut-leaved Toothwort	*Dentaria laciniata*
Daisy	*Chrysanthemum leucanthemum* and others
Duckweed	*Lemna* spp.
Dutchman's-breeches	*Dicentra cucullaria*
Dwarf Larkspur	*Delphinium tricorne*
Early Saxifrage	*Saxifraga virginiensis*
Ebony Spleenwort	*Asplenium platyneuron*
Fern, Bulblet	*Cystopteris bulbifera*
Fern, Lip	*Cheilanthes lanosa*
Fern, Ostrich	*Matteuccia struthiopteris*
Fern, Polypody	*Polypodium virginianum*
Fern, Walking	*Camptosorus rhizophyllus*
Floating Paspalum	*Paspalum fluitans*
Gill-over-the-ground	*Glechoma hederacea*
Goldenrod, Riverbank	*Solidago racemosa*
Goldenrod, Shale	*S. arguta* variety
Hairy Wild Petunia	*Ruellia humilis*
Halberd-leaved Rose Mallow	*Hibiscus laevis*
Harbinger-of-spring	*Erigenia bulbosa*
Hispid Buttercup	*Ranunculus hispidus*
Indiangrass	*Sorghastrum nutans*
Jewel-weed	*Impatiens capensis*
Kates Mountain Clover	*Trifolium virginicum*
Least Duckweed	*Lemna minor*
Lizard's-tail	*Saururus cernuus*

Common Name	Scientific Name
May-apple	*Podophyllum peltatum*
Milkvetch, Bent	*Astragalus distortus*
Milkvetch, Canada	*A. canadensis*
Mistflower	*Eupatorium coelestinum*
Miterwort	*Mitella diphylla*
Morning Glory, Ivy-leaved	*Ipomoea hederacea*
Morning Glory, Shale Barren	*Ipomoea sp.*
Narrow Melic Grass	*Melica mutica*
Periwinkle	*Vinca minor*
Phlox, Moss (Moss Pink)	*Phlox subulata*
Phlox, Wild Blue	*P. divaricata*
Pondweed	*Potamogeton* spp.
Prickly Pear	*Opuntia humifusa*
Purple Cliffbrake	*Pellaea atropurpurea*
Pussytoes	*Antennaria sp.*
Pussytoes, Shale Barren	*Antennaria sp.*
Ragwort	*Senecio sp.*
Ragwort, Golden	*S. aureus*
Ragwort, Round-leaved	*S. obovatus*
Ragwort, Shale Barren	*S. antennariifolius*
Ramp	*Allium tricoccum*
Rock Cress	*Arabis sp.*
Rocktwist	*Draba ramosissima*
Skullcap, Dwarf	*Scutellaria sp.*
Skullcap, Rock	*S. saxitilis*
Sedum	*Sedum ternatum*
Shale Evening-primrose	*Oenothera argillicola*
Shooting Star	*Dodecatheon meadia*
Spatterdock	*Nuphar advena*
Spring Beauty	*Claytonia virginica*
Squirrel-corn	*Dicentra canadensis*
Star-flowered False Solomon's-seal	*Smilicina stellata*
Stinging Nettle	*Urtica dioica*
Trailing Arbutus	*Epigaea repens*
Trillium, Sessile	*Trillium sessile*
Trillium, Snow	*T. nivale*
Trout-lily, White	*Erythronium albidum*
Trout-lily, Yellow	*E. americanum*
Twinleaf	*Jeffersonia diphylla*
Violet, Birdfoot	*Viola pedata*
Violet, Green	*Hybanthus concolor*
Violet, Pale	*Viola striata*
Virginia Bluebell	*Mertensia virginica*
Virginia Dayflower	*Commelina virginica*
Wake-robin	*Trillium erectum*
Wall Rue	*Asplenium cryptolepis*
Water-cress	*Nasturtium officinale*
Water Stargrass	*Heteranthera dubia*
Water Willow	*Justicia americana*
Wild False Indigo	*Baptisia australis*
Wild Ginger	*Asarum canadense*
Wild Oat	*Uvularia sessilifolia*
Wild Stonecrop (see Sedum)	
Yellow Passionflower	*Passiflora lutea*

Trees, Shrubs, and Vines

This list contains species of woody plants that have been found or are to be expected within the C & O Canal National Historical Park. It is based primarily on Terrell, Spring flora of the Chesapeake and Ohio Canal area, Washington, D.C., to Seneca, Maryland (Castanea 35(1), 1970); Brown and Brown, *Woody Plants of Maryland*, 1972; Little, *Atlas of United States Trees*, 1971; and my own records. Species not recorded but to be expected in the area are marked with an asterisk. Non-native species are marked with a plus sign. Scientific names follow Fernald, *Gray's Manual of Botany*, 8th ed., 1950.

Common Name	Scientific Name	Form (Tree, Shrub, Vine)
Pitch Pine	Pinus rigida	T
*Shortleaf Pine	P. echinata	T
Table Mountain Pine	P. pungens	T
Eastern White Pine	P. strobes	T
Virginia Pine	P. virginiana	T
Red Cedar	Juniperus virginiana	T
Hemlock	Tsuga Canadensis	T
Northern White-cedar	Thuja occidentalis	T
*Glaucous Greenbrier	Smilax glauca	V
Catbrier	S. rotundifolia	V
Eastern Cottonwood	Populus deltoides	T
*Large-toothed Aspen	P. grandidentata	T
+Weeping Willow	Salix babylonica	T
Ward's Willow	S. caroliniana	S,T
Black Willow	S. nigra	S,T
*Sandbar Willow	S. interior	S
*Heartleaf Willow	S. rigida	S
*Prairie Willow	S. humilis	S
*Silky Willow	S. sericea	S
Bitternut Hickory	Carya cordiformis	T
*Shagbark Hickory	C. ovata	T
Mockernut Hickory	C. tomentosa	T
Pignut Hickory	C. glabra	T
*Sweet Pignut Hickory	C. ovalis	T
*Butternut	Juglans cinerea	T
Black Walnut	J. nigra	T
Sweet Gum	Liquidambar styraciflua	T
Common Alder	Alnus serrulata	S
*Black Birch	Betula lenta	T
River Birch	B. nigra	T
American Hornbeam	Carpinus caroliniana	T
Hazelnut	Corylus Americana	S
Ironwood	Ostrya virginiana	T
Chestnut	Castanea dentata	T
Beech	Fagus grandifolia	T
White Oak	Quercus alba	T
Swamp White Oak	Q. bicolor	T
Chinquapin Oak	Q. muehlenbergii	T
Northern Red Oak	Q. rubra	T
Scarlet Oak	Q. coccinea	T
Southern Red Oak	Q. falcata	T
Scrub Oak	Q. ilicifolia	S,T
*Blackjack Oak	Q. marilandica	T,S
Shingle Oak	Q. imbricaria	T

Common Name	Scientific Name	Form (Tree, Shrub, Vine)
Pin Oak	*Q. palustris*	T
Willow Oak	*Q. phellos*	T
Chestnut Oak	*Q. prinus*	T
Shumard Oak	*Q. shumardii*	T
Post Oak	*Q. stellata*	T
Black Oak	*Q. velutina*	T
American Hackberry	*Celtis occidentalis*	T
American Elm	*Ulmus Americana*	T
Slippery Elm	*U. rubra*	T
+Paper Mulberry	*Broussonetia papyrifera*	T
+Osage Orange	*Maclura pomifera*	T
+White Mulberry	*Morus alba*	T
Red Mulberry	*M. rubra*	T
Virgin's-bower	*Clematis virginiana*	V
Leather Flower	*C. viorna*	V
+Japanese Barberry	*Berberis thunbergii*	S
Canada Moonseed	*Menispermum canadense*	V
Cucumber Tree	*Magnolia acuminata*	T
Tuliptree	*Liriodendron tulipifera*	T
Paw Paw	*Asimina triloba*	T
Spicebush	*Lindera benzoin*	S
Sassafras	*Sassafras albidum*	T
Wild Hydrangea	*Hydrangea arborescens*	S
*Wild Black Currant	*Ribes americanum*	S
Witch-hazel	*Hamamelis virginiana*	S
Sycamore	*Platanus occidentalis*	T
Ninebark	*Physocarpus opulifolius*	S
*Narrow-leaved Meadowsweet	*Spiraea alba*	S
*Steeplebush	*S. tomentosa*	S
*Dwarf Spiraea	*S. corymbosa*	S
Red Chokeberry	*Pyrus arbutifolia*	S
*Wild Crab	*P. coronaria*	T
Downy Serviceberry	*Amelanchier arborea*	S,T
Smooth Serviceberry	*A. laevis*	S,T
Round-leaved Serviceberry	*A. humilis*	S
Hawthorn	*Crataegus* spp.	T,S
One-flowered Hawthorn	*C. uniflora*	S
Wild Plum	*Prunus Americana*	S,T
+Sweet Cherry	*P. avium*	T
Black Cherry	*P. serotina*	T
+Multiflora Rose	*Rosa multiflora*	S
*Pasture Rose	*R. virginiana*	S
*Swamp Rose	*R. palustris*	S
Low Pasture Rose	*R. Carolina*	S
Blackberry	*Rubus* spp.	S
Wineberry	*R. phoenicolasius*	S
Honey-locust	*Gleditsia triacanthos*	T
Redbud	*Cercis Canadensis*	T
Black Locust	*Robinia pseudo-acacia*	T
Hop Tree	*Ptelea trifoliata*	S,T
Tree of Heaven	*Ailanthus altissima*	T
Dwarf Sumac	*Rhus copallina*	S,T
Smooth Sumac	*R. glabra*	S
Fragrant Sumac	*R. aromatica*	S
Poison-ivy	*R. radicans*	S,V
Staghorn Sumac	*R. typhina*	S,T
Deciduous Holly	*Ilex decidua*	T,S
American Holly	*I. opaca*	T
Bittersweet	*Celastrus scandens*	S
Winged Euonymus	*Euonymus alatus*	S
Strawberry-bush	*E. americanus*	S

148

Common Name	Scientific Name	Form (Tree, Shrub, Vine)
Wahoo	*E. atropurpureus*	S,T
Bladdernut	*Staphylea trifolia*	S,T
Boxelder	*Acer negundo*	T
Red Maple	*A. rubrum*	T
Silver Maple	*A. saccharinum*	T
Sugar Maple	*A. saccharum*	T
Black Maple	*A. nigrum*	T
Prairie Redroot	*Ceanothus ovatus*	S
New Jersey Tea	*C. americanus*	S
Virginia Creeper	*Parthenocissus quinquefolia*	V
Riverbank Grape	*Vitis riparia*	V
Frost Grape	*V. vulpine*	V
*Fox Grape	*V. labrusca*	V
*Summer Grape	*V. aestivalis*	V
*Sand Grape	*V. rupestris*	V
American Basswood	*Tilia Americana*	T
White Basswood	*T. heterophylla*	T
Shrubby St. Johnswort	*Hypericum spathulatum*	S
*Leatherwood	*Dirca palustris*	S
Black Gum	*Nyssa sylvatica*	T
*Hercules-club	*Aralia spinosa*	S,T
+English Ivy	*Hedera helix*	S,V
Silky Dogwood	*Cornus amomum*	S
Flowering Dogwood	*C. florida*	T
*Paniculate Dogwood	*C. racemosa*	S
Spotted Wintergreen	*Chimaphila maculata*	S
Pipsissewa	*C. umbellata*	S
Trailing Arbutus	*Epigaea repens*	S
*Teaberry	*Gaultheria procumbens*	S
Swamp Sweetbells	*Leucothoe racemosa*	S
Black Huckleberry	*Gaylusaccia baccata*	S
Mountain Laurel	*Kalmia latifolia*	S
Rosebay Rhododendron	*Rhododendron maximum*	S
Pinxter-flower	*R. nudiflorum*	S
*Swamp Azalea	*R. viscosum*	S
*Maleberry	*Lyonia ligustrina*	S
Deerberry	*Vaccinium stamineum*	S
Low Blueberry	*V. vacillans*	S
*Low Sweet Blueberry	*V. angustifolium*	S
Persimmon	*Diospyros virginiana*	T
Fringe Tree	*Chionanthus virginicus*	S,T
White Ash	*Fraxinus Americana*	T
Green Ash	*F. pennsylvanica*	T
Privet	*Ligustrum vulgare*	S
+Princess Tree	*Paulownia tomentosa*	T
Trumpet Creeper	*Campsis radicans*	V
Buttonbush	*Cephalanthus occidentalis*	S
Partridgeberry	*Mitchella repens*	S
+Japanese Honeysuckle	*Lonicera japonica*	S,V
Mountain Honeysuckle	*L. dioica*	S
+Tartarian Honeysuckle	*L. tatarica*	S
Bush Honeysuckle	*Diervilla lonicera*	S
Common Elderberry	*Sambucus Canadensis*	S
Maple-leaved Viburnum	*Viburnum acerifolium*	S
Black-haw	*V. prunifolium*	S
Downy Arrowwood	*V. rafinesquianum*	S
*Smooth Arrowwood	*V. recognitum*	S

Butterflies

The following species were recorded in or immediately adjacent to the C & O Canal National Historical Park during surveys by Stephanie Mason and Mark Garland (D.C., Montgomery, and Frederick counties) and by Ed Thompson (Washington and Allegany counties). These counties are indicated here as D, M, F, W, A

Common Name	Scientific Name	Location
Pipevine Swallowtail	Battus philenor	M, A
Zebra Swallowtail	Eurytides marcellus	D, M, F, W, A
Black Swallowtail	Papilio polyxenes	D, F, A
Giant Swallowtail	P. cresphontes	M, A
Tiger Swallowtail	P. glaucus	D, M, F, W, A
Spicebush Swallowtail	P. troilus	D, M, F, W, A
Cabbage White	Pieris rapae	D, M, F, W, A
Clouded Sulphur	Colias philodice	D, M, F, W, A
Orange Sulphur	C. eurytheme	D, M, F, W, A
Little Sulphur	Eurema lisa	A
Sleepy Orange	E. nicippe	M
Falcate Orange Tip	Anthocharis midea	W, A
Olympia Marble	Euchloe olympia	A
Little Copper	Lycaena phlaeas	W, A
Banded Hairstreak	Satyrium calanus	M, F, A
Striped Hairstreak	S. liparops	M, A
Coral Hairstreak	S. titus	A
Red-banded Hairstreak	Calycopis cecrops	M
Olive Hairstreak	Mitoura grynea grynea	A
White-M Hairstreak	Parrhasius m-album	M, F
Gray Hairstreak	Strymon melinus	D, M, F, A
Henry's Elfin	Incisalia henrici	A
Silvery Blue	Glaucopsyche lygdamus	W, A
Eastern Tailed Blue	Everes comyntas	D, M, F, W, A
Appalachian Blue	Celastrina neglecta-major	W, A
Spring Azure	Celastrina ladon	D, M, F, W, A
Northern Metalmark	Calephalis borealis	W, A
Snout Butterfly	Libytheana carinenta	M, F, A
Variegated Fritillary	Euptoieta claudia	D, M, F
Great Spangled Fritillary	Speyeria cybele	D, M, F, W, A
Aphrodite Fritillary	S. Aphrodite	A
Meadow Fritillary	Boloria bellona	M, F
Silvery Checkerspot	Chlosyne nycteis	M, F
Pearl Crescent	Phyciodes tharos	D, M, F, W, A
Question Mark	Polygonia interrogationis	D, M, F, W, A
Eastern Comma	P. comma	D, M, F, W, A
Mourning Cloak	Nymphalis antiopa	M, F, W, A
American Painted Lady	Vanessa virginiensis	D, M, F, A
Painted Lady	V. cardui	W, A
Red Admiral	V. atalanta	D, M, F, W, A
Buckeye	Junonia coenia	D, M, F
Red-spotted Purple	Limenitis arthemis astyanax	D, M, F, W, A
Viceroy	L. archippus	D, F
Hackberry Butterfly	Asterocampa celtis	M, F, W, A
Tawny Emperor	A. clyton	M, F, W, A
Northern Pearly Eye	Enodia anthedon	D, M, A
Appalachian Eyed Brown	Satyrodes appalachia	M, A

Common Name	Scientific Name	Location
Little Wood Satyr	*Megisto cymela*	M, F, W, A
Common Wood Nymph	*Cercyonis pegala*	M, A
Monarch	*Danaus plexippus*	D, M, F, A
Silver-spotted Skipper	*Epargyreus clarus*	D, M, F, W, A
Hoary Edge	*Achalarus lyciades*	M
Northern Cloudywing	*Thorybes pylades*	M, A
Scalloped Sootywing	*Staphylus hayhurstii*	M, F
Sleepy Duskywing	*Erynnis brizo*	A
Juvenal's Duskywing	*E. juvenalis*	W, A
Horace's Duskywing	*E. horatius*	D, M
Wild Indigo Duskywing	*E. baptisiae*	D, M, F
Dreamy Duskywing	*E. icelus*	A
Checkered Skipper	*Pyrgus communis*	D, M, F, A
Leonard's Skipper	*Hesperia leonardus*	A
Common Sootywing	*Pholisora catullus*	F, A
Swarthy Skipper	*Nastra lherminier*	D, M, F
Clouded Skipper	*Lerema accius*	D, F
Least Skipper	*Ancyloxpha numitor*	D, M, F
European Skipper	*Thymelicus lineola*	D, F
Fiery Skipper	*Hylephila phyleus*	D, M, F
Peck's Skipper	*Polites peckius*	M, F
Tawny-edged Skipper	*P. themistocles*	M, F
Crossline Skipper	*P. origenes*	D, M, F
Long Dash	*P. mystic*	A
Northern Broken Dash	*Wallengrenia egeremet*	M, F
Roadside Skipper	*Ambylscirtes vialis*	A
Little Glassywing	*Pompeius verna*	M, F
Sachem	*Atalopedes campestris*	D, M, F
Hobomok Skipper	*Poanes hobomok*	M, A
Zabulon Skipper	*P. zabulon*	D, M, F
Dun Skipper	*Euphyes vestries*	M, F
Ocola Skipper	*Panoquina ocola*	D

Fishes

The following species were recorded in the C & O Canal National Historical Park during a survey by Richard L. Raesly, Department of Biology, Frostburg State University, in 2002. The waters sampled were the canal and streams passing through the park. The Potomac River is outside the park boundaries and was not sampled.

Common Name	Scientific Name
American Eel	*Anguilla rostrata*
Stoneroller	*Campostoma anomalum*
Goldfish	*Carassius auratus*
Rosyside Dace	*Clinostomus funduloides*
	Cyprinella anlostana
	C. spiloptera
Carp	*Cyprinus carpio*
Cutlips Minnow	*Exoglossum maxillingua*
	Hybognathus regius

Common Name	Scientific Name
	Luxilus cornutus
	Margariscus margarita
River Chub	Nocomis micropogon
Golden Shiner	Notemigonus crysoleucus
Comely Shiner	Notropis amoenus
	N. buccatus
Spottail Shiner	N. hudsonius
Swallowtail Shiner	N. procne
Rosyface Shiner	N. rubellus
Bluntnose Minnow	Pimephales notatus
Fathead Minnow	P. promelas
Blacknose Dace	Rhinichthys aratulus
	R. cateractae
Creek Chub	Semotilus atromaculatus
Fallfish	S. corporalis
White Sucker	Catostomus commersoni
Creek Chubsucker	Erimyzon oblongus
Northern Hog Sucker	Hypentelium nigricans
Golden Redhorse	Moxostoma erythrurum
Yellow Bullhead	Ameiurus natalis
Brown Bullhead	A. nebulosus
White Catfish	A. catus
Channel Catfish	Ictalurus punctatus
Margined Madtom	Noturus insignis
Chain Pickerel	Esox niger
	Umbra pygmaea
Rainbow Trout	Oncorhynchus mykiss
Brown Trout	Salmo trutta
Brook Trout	Salvelinus fontinalis
	Gambusia holbrooki
	Cottus caeruleomentum
Potomac Sculpin	C. girardi
	C. sp. cf. cognatus
Rock Bass	Ambloplites rupestris
Redbreast Sunfish	Lepomis auritus
Green Sunfish	L. cyanellus
Pumpkinseed	L. gibbosus
Warmouth	L. gulosus
Bluegill	L. macrochirus
Longear Sunfish	L. megalotis
	Lepomis hybrids
Smallmouth Bass	Micropterus dolomieu
Largemouth Bass	M. salmoides
White Crappie	Pomoxis annularis

Common Name	Scientific Name
Black Crappie	*P. nigromaculatus*
Greenside Darter	*Etheostoma blennioides*
Rainbow Darter	*E. caeruleum*
Fantail Darter	*E. flabellare*
Tessellated Darter	*E. olmstedi*
Shield Darter	*Percina peltata*
Yellow Perch	*Perca flavescens*
Walleye	*Stizostedion vitreum*

Reptiles and Amphibians

This list is based largely on distribution maps in *Checklist of Reptiles and Amphibians of Maryland*, by Herbert S. Harris, Jr., 1969, and on consultation with Mr. Harris and Ed Thompson, Maryland Department of Natural Resources. Counties in which a species has been recorded in or close to the park are indicated by capital letters: M – Montgomery Co.; F – Frederick Co.; W – Washington Co.; A – Allegany Co. Parentheses indicate that the species was recorded from the county but not close to the park. An asterisk means that the species probably exists in the park but no record has been obtained.

Common Name	Scientific Name	Location
Red-spotted Newt	*Notophthalmus v. viridescens*	M,F,W,A
Jefferson Salamander	*Ambystoma jeffersonianum*	F,W,A
Spotted Salamander	*A. maculatum*	M,F,W,A
Marbled Salamander	*A. opacum*	M,(F),W,A
Northern Two-lined Salamander	*Eurycea b. bislineata*	M,F,W,A
Long-tailed Salamander	*E. l. longicauda*	M,F,W,A
Four-toed Salamander	*Hemidactylium scutatum*	M W,A
Red-backed Salamander	*Plethodon c. cinereus*	M,F,W,(A)
Valley and Ridge Salamander	*P. hoffmani*	W,A
Slimy Salamander	*P. g. glutinosus*	M,F,W,A
*Northern Spring Salamander	*Gyrinophilus p. porphyriticus*	(F) (A)
Eastern Mud Salamander	*Pseudotriton m. montanus*	M
Northern Red Salamander	*P. r. ruber*	M,(F),W,A
Northern Dusky Salamander	*Desmognathus f. fuscus*	M,F,W,A
American Toad	*Bufo a. americanus*	M,F,W,A
Fowler's Toad	*B. woodhousei fowleri*	M,(F),W,A
Northern Cricket Frog	*Acris c. crepitans*	M,(F),W,A
Northern Spring Peeper	*Hyla c. crucifer*	M,F,W,A
Eastern Gray Treefrog	*H. v. versicolor*	M,(F), A
Upland Chorus Frog	*Pseudacris triseriata feriarum*	M,(F),W,A
Bullfrog	*Rana catesbeiana*	M,(F),W,A
Green Frog	*R. clamitans melanota*	M,F,W,A
Pickerel Frog	*R. palustris*	M,F,W,A
Wood Frog	*R. s. sylvatica*	M,F,W,A
Northern Fence Lizard	*Sceloporus undulates hyacinthinus*	M,(F),W,A
Six-lined Racerunner	*Cnemidophorus sexlineatus*	A

Common Name	Scientific Name	Location
Five-lined Skink	*Eumeces fasciatus*	M,(F),W,(A)
Broad-headed Skink	*E. laticeps*	M,(F)
Eastern Worm Snake	*Carphophis a. amoenus*	M,(F),W,A
Northern Ringnecked Snake	*Diadophis punctatus edwardsi*	M,(F),W,A
Eastern Hognose Snake	*Heterodon platyrhinos*	M,(F),W,A
Rough Green Snake	*Opheodrys aestivus*	M
Eastern Smooth Green Snake	*O. v. vernalis*	(F),W,(A)
Northern Black Racer	*Coluber c. constrictor*	M,F,W,A
Black Rat Snake	*Elaphe o. obsoleta*	M,F,W,A
Corn Snake	*E. g. guttata*	A
*Eastern Kingsnake	*Lampropeltis g. getulus*	(M)
Eastern Milk Snake	*L. t. triangulum*	M,(F),W,A
Northern Water Snake	*Nerodia s. sipedon*	M,F,W,A
Queen Snake	*Regina s. septemvittata*	M,(F), (A)
Northern Brown Snake	*Storeria d. dekayi*	M,(F),(W),A
Northern Red-bellied Snake	*S. o. occipitomaculata*	(F),W,A
Eastern Earth Snake	*Virginia v. valeriae*	M,(F),W,A
Eastern Ribbon Snake	*Thamnophis s. sauritus*	M,(F),W,(A)
Eastern Garter Snake	*T. s. sirtalis*	M,F,W,A
Northern Copperhead	*Agkistrodon contortrix mokeson*	M,(F),W,A
Timber Rattlesnake	*Crotalus h. horridus*	(F),W,A
Stinkpot (Musk Turtle)	*Sternothaerus odoratus*	M,F,W,A
Eastern Mud Turtle	*Kinosternum s. subrubrum*	M
Snapping Turtle	*Chelydra s. serpentina*	M,F,W,A
Spotted Turtle	*Clemmys guttata*	M,F,W
Wood Turtle	*Glyptemys insculpta*	M,(F),W,A
Eastern Box Turtle	*Terrapene c. carolina*	M,F,W,A
Eastern Painted Turtle	*Chrysemys p. picta*	M,F,W,A
Red-bellied Turtle	*Pseudemys rubiventris*	M,(F),W,A

Birds

The following list contains all species recorded in or immediately adjacent to the national historical park. It is based on Byron Swift's leaflet, "Birds Along the C & O Canal," with additional input from *Field List of the Birds of Maryland* (May 1996), *Atlas of the Breeding Birds of Maryland and the District of Columbia* (1996), and the records of the late Jim Paulus, Chandler Robbins, myself, and other birders. Seasons: Sp – Spring (April-May); Su – Summer (June-August 15); F – Fall (August 16-November); W – Winter (December-March). Abundance: C – Common; F – Fairly Common; U – Uncommon; R – Rare. Notes: N – north of Harpers Ferry; S – south of Harpers Ferry; L – local. Abundance within the park may be different from that outside the park because of restriction of certain habitats in the park.

Species	Sp	Su	F	W	Notes
Common Loon	U		U	R	
Red-throated Loon	R			R	
Red-necked Grebe	R		R	R	
Horned Grebe	U		U	U	
Pied-billed Grebe	U	R	U	U	
Double-crested Cormorant	C	U	C		

Species	Sp	Su	F	W	Notes
Great Blue Heron	C	C	C	U	
Green Heron	C	C	C		
Little Blue Heron		R	R		
Great Egret	F	U	U		
Snowy Egret		R	R		
Cattle Egret		R	R		
Black-crowned Night Heron	U	U	U		
Yellow-crowned Night Heron	R	R	R		
Least Bittern	R	R	R		
American Bittern	R	R	R		
Tundra Swan	U		U	R	
Snow Goose	R		R	R	
Canada Goose	C	F	C	C	
Mallard	C	C	C	C	
American Black Duck	U		U	U	
Gadwall	R		R	R	
Northern Pintail	R		R	R	
Green-winged Teal	U		U	U	
Blue-winged Teal	F		U		
American Wigeon	U		U	U	
Northern Shoveler	R		R	R	
Wood Duck	F	F	F	U	
Redhead	R		R	R	
Ring-necked Duck	U		U	U	
Canvasback	U		U	U	
Greater Scaup	R		R	R	
Lesser Scaup	U		U	U	
Common Goldeneye	U		U	U	
Bufflehead	U		U	U	
Long-tailed Duck	R		R	R	
White-winged Scoter	R		R		
Ruddy Duck	U		U	U	
Hooded Merganser	U	R	U	U	
Common Merganser	U		U	U	
Red-breasted Merganser	U		U	U	
Turkey Vulture	C	C	C	C	
Black Vulture	U	U	U	U	
Sharp-shinned Hawk	U	R	F	U	
Cooper's Hawk	R	R	R	R	
Northern Goshawk	R		R	R	
Red-tailed Hawk	C	C	C	C	
Red-shouldered Hawk	C	C	C	C	
Broad-winged Hawk	F	U	F		
Rough-legged Hawk	R		R	R	
Golden Eagle	R		R	R	
Bald Eagle	U	U	U	U	
Northern Harrier	R		R	R	
Osprey	U	R	U		
Peregrine Falcon	R		R		
Merlin	R		R		
American Kestrel	U	U	U	U	
Ruffed Grouse	U	U	U	U	N
Northern Bobwhite	U	U	U	U	
Ring-necked Pheasant	U	U	U	U	
Wild Turkey	U	U	U	U	
King Rail	R		R		
Sora	U		U		
Virginia Rail	R		R		
Purple Gallinule		R			
Common Moorhen	U		U		
American Coot	U		U	U	

Species	Sp	Su	F	W	Notes
Semipalmated Plover	R		R		
Killdeer	U	U	U	U	
American Golden-Plover		R	R		L
Black-bellied Plover	R	R	R		L
American Woodcock	U	U	U	R	
Wilson's Snipe	U		U	U	
Upland Sandpiper	U	U	U		L
Spotted Sandpiper	F	U	F		
Solitary Sandpiper	F	U	F		
Greater Yellowlegs	R		R		
Lesser Yellowlegs	U	U	U		
Pectoral Sandpiper	U	U	U		L
Least Sandpiper	U	U	U		L
Buff-breasted Sandpiper		R	R		L
Dunlin			R		L
Short-billed Dowitcher		R	R		L
Long-billed Dowitcher			R		L
Stilt Sandpiper			R		L
White-rumped Sandpiper			R		L
Semipalmated Sandpiper	R	R	R		L
Western Sandpiper	R	R	R		L
Baird's Sandpiper		R	R		L
Sanderling			R		L
Wilson's Phalarope			R		L
Northern Phalarope			R		L
Great Black-backed Gull	U	R	U	U	S
Herring Gull	U	R	U	U	
Ring-billed Gull	C	U	C	C	
Laughing Gull		U	U		S
Bonaparte's Gull	U	R	R		
Common Tern	R		R		
Caspian Tern	U	U	U		
Forster's Tern	U	U	U		
Black Tern	R		R		
Rock Pigeon	C	C	C	C	
Mourning Dove	C	C	C	C	
Yellow-billed Cuckoo	C	C	C		
Black-billed Cuckoo	U	U	U		
Barn Owl	U	U	U	U	
Eastern Screech-Owl	F	F	F	F	
Great Horned Owl	U	U	U	U	
Barred Owl	C	C	C	C	
Long-eared Owl				R	
Short-eared Owl				R	
Northern Saw-whet Owl				R	
Whip-poor-will	U	U	U		
Chuck-will's-widow	R		R		
Common Nighthawk	U	U	U		
Chimney Swift	C	C	C		
Ruby-throated Hummingbird	F	F	F		
Belted Kingfisher	F	F	F	F	
Northern Flicker	C	C	C	C	
Pileated Woodpecker	C	C	C	C	
Red-bellied Woodpecker	C	C	C	C	
Red-headed Woodpecker	R	R	R	R	L
Yellow-bellied Sapsucker	U		U	U	
Hairy Woodpecker	F	F	F	F	
Downy Woodpecker	C	C	C	C	
Eastern Kingbird	C	C	C		
Great Crested Flycatcher	C	C	C		
Eastern Phoebe	C	C	C	R	

Species	Sp	Su	F	W	Notes
Yellow-bellied Flycatcher	U		U		
Acadian Flycatcher	C	C	C		
Alder Flycatcher	R		R		
Willow Flycatcher	U	R	U		
Least Flycatcher	U		U		
Eastern Wood-Pewee	C	C	C		
Olive-sided Flycatcher	R		R		
Horned Lark	R	R	R	R	
Tree Swallow	C	C	C		
Bank Swallow	F	U	F		
Northern Rough-winged Swallow	C	C	C		
Barn Swallow	C	C	C		
Cliff Swallow	U	R	U		
Purple Martin	U	U			
Blue Jay	C	C	C	C	
Common Raven	U	U	U	U	
American Crow	C	C	C	C	
Fish Crow	C	C	C	C	
Black-capped Chickadee	C	C	C	C	N
Carolina Chickadee	C	C	C	C	
Tufted Titmouse	C	C	C	C	
White-breasted Nuthatch	C	F	C	C	
Red-breasted Nuthatch	U		U	U	
Brown Creeper	U	R	U	U	
House Wren	C	C	C	R	
Winter Wren	U		U	U	
Bewick's Wren	R	R	R		N
Sedge Wren	R	R	R		
Marsh Wren	U	U	U	R	S
Carolina Wren	C	C	C	C	
Northern Mockingbird	C	C	C	C	
Gray Catbird	C	C	C	R	
Brown Thrasher	U	U	U	R	
American Robin	C	C	C	U	
Wood Thrush	C	C	C		
Hermit Thrush	U		U	U	
Swainson's Thrush	C		C		
Gray-cheeked Thrush	U		U		
Veery	C	U	C		
Eastern Bluebird	C	U	C	C	
Blue-gray Gnatcatcher	C	C	C		
Golden-crowned Kinglet	C		C	C	
Ruby-crowned Kinglet	C		C	U	
American Pipit	U		U	U	
Cedar Waxwing	F	U	F	F	
Loggerhead Shrike	R		R	R	
European Starling	C	C	C	C	
White-eyed Vireo	F	F	F		
Yellow-throated Vireo	U	U	U		
Blue-headed Vireo	U		U		
Red-eyed Vireo	C	C	C		
Philadelphia Vireo	R		R		
Warbling Vireo	F	F	F		
Black and White Warbler	C	U	C		
Prothonotary Warbler	C	C	U		
Worm-eating Warbler	U	U	U		
Golden-winged Warbler	U	R	U		
Blue-winged Warbler	F	R	F		
Tennessee Warbler	C		C		
Orange-crowned Warbler	R		R		
Nashville Warbler	F		U		

Species	Sp	Su	F	W	Notes
Northern Parula	C	C	C		
Yellow Warbler	C	C	C		
Magnolia Warbler	F		F		
Cape May Warbler	F		F		
Black-throated Blue Warbler	F		F		
Yellow-rumped Warbler	C		C	C	
Black-throated Green Warbler	F		F		
Cerulean Warbler	U	U	U		
Blackburnian Warbler	U		U		
Yellow-throated Warbler	U	U	U		
Chestnut-sided Warbler	F		F		
Bay-breasted Warbler	U		U		
Blackpoll Warbler	C		C		
Pine Warbler	U	U	U		
Prairie Warbler	U	U	U		
Palm Warbler	U		U	R	
Ovenbird	C	C	C		
Northern Waterthrush	F		F		
Louisiana Waterthrush	F	F	F		
Kentucky Warbler	U	U	U		
Connecticut Warbler	R		R		
Mourning Warbler	R		R		
Common Yellowthroat	C	C	C	R	
Yellow-breasted Chat	F	F	F		
Hooded Warbler	U	R	U		
Wilson's Warbler	U		U		
Canada Warbler	F		F		
American Redstart	C	F	C		
Scarlet Tanager	C	C	C		
Summer Tanager	U	R	U		
Northern Cardinal	C	C	C	C	
Rose-breasted Grosbeak	F	R			
Blue Grosbeak	U	U	U		
Indigo Bunting	C	C	C		
Dickcissel	R	R	R		
Eastern Towhee	C	C	C	U	
Savannah Sparrow	U	?	U		
Grasshopper Sparrow	U	U	U		L
Henslow's Sparrow	R	?	R		L
Vesper Sparrow	U	?	U		
American Tree Sparrow				U	
Chipping Sparrow	C	F	C	R	
Field Sparrow	F	F	F	U	
White-crowned Sparrow	U		U	U	
White-throated Sparrow	C		C	C	
Fox Sparrow	U		U	U	
Lincoln's Sparrow	R		U		
Swamp Sparrow	F	R	F	F	
Song Sparrow	C	C	C	C	
Dark-eyed Junco	C		C	C	
Lapland Longspur			R		L
Snow Bunting			R		
Bobolink	U		U		
Eastern Meadowlark	U	U	U	R	
Red-winged Blackbird	C	C	C	U	
Orchard Oriole	C	F	C		
Baltimore Oriole	C	C	C		
Rusty Blackbird	R		F	U	
Common Grackle	C	C	C	U	
Brown-headed Cowbird	C	C	C	U	
Purple Finch	C		C	C	

Species	Sp	Su	F	W	Notes
House Finch	U	U	U	U	
Common Redpoll				R	
Red Crossbill				R	
White-winged Crossbill				R	
Pine Siskin	U		U	U	
American Goldfinch	C	C	C	C	
Evening Grosbeak	R		R	R	
House Sparrow	C	C	C	C	

Vagrants (outside normal range)

American White Pelican
Anhinga
Tricolored Heron
Glossy Ibis
White Ibis
Fulvous Whistling-Duck
Surf Scoter
Swallow-tailed Kite
Sharp-tailed Sandpiper
Red Phalarope

Ruddy Turnstone
Willet
American Avocet
Iceland Gull
Swainson's Warbler
Black-headed Grosbeak
Bachman's Sparrow
Brewer's Blackbird

Mammals

This list is based largely on *Mammals of Maryland*, by John Paradiso, 1969. All species have been recorded in or immediately adjacent to the park except for those marked with an asterisk, which are probable because of their normal range and habitat preference.

Common Name	Scientific Name
Opossum	*Didelphis marsupialis virginiana*
Masked Shrew	*Sorex cinereus*
Short-tailed Shrew	*Blarina brevicauda kirtlandi*
*Least Shrew	*Cryptotis parva parva*
Eastern Mole	*Scalopus aquaticus aquaticus*
Starnosed Mole	*Condylura cristata cristata*
Little Brown Bat	*Myotis lucifugus lucifugus*
Keen's Bat	*M. keenii septendrionalis*
Indiana Bat	*M. sodalis*
Small-footed Bat	*M. subulatus leibii*
Silver-haired Bat	*Lasionycteris noctivagans*
Eastern Pipistrelle	*Pipistrellus subflavus subflavus*
Big Brown Bat	*Eptesicus fuscus fuscus*
Red Bat	*Lasiurus borealis borealis*
*Hoary Bat	*L. cinereus cinereus*
Evening Bat	*Nycticeius humeralis humeralis*
Eastern Cottontail	*Sylvilagus floridanus mallurus*
Eastern Chipmunk	*Tamias striatus*
Woodchuck	*Marmota monax monax*
Gray Squirrel	*Sciurus caroliniensis pennsylvanicus*

Common Name	Scientific Name
Fox Squirrel	*S. niger*
Red Squirrel	*Tamiasciurus hudsonicus loquax*
Southern Flying Squirrel	*Glaucomys volans volans*
Beaver	*Castor canadensis*
White-footed Mouse	*Peromyscus leucopus noveboracensis*
Deer Mouse	*P. maniculatus*
Alleghany Woodrat	*Neotoma magister*
Meadow Vole	*Microtus pennsylvanicus*
Pine Vole	*Pitymys pinetorum scalopsoides*
Muskrat	*Ondatra zibethicus*
Norway (Brown) Rat	*Rattus norvegicus*
House Mouse	*Mus musculus*
Meadow Jumping Mouse	*Zapus hudsonius americanus*
Woodland Jumping Mouse	*Napaeozapus insignis*
Red Fox	*Vulpes fulva fulva*
Gray Fox	*Urocyon cinereoargenteus cinereoargenteus*
Coyote	*Canis latrans*
Black Bear	*Ursus americanus*
Raccoon	*Procyon lotor lotor*
Long-tailed Weasel	*Mustela frenata noveboracensis*
Mink	*M. vison mink*
Striped Skunk	*Mephitis mephitis nigra*
River Otter	*Lutra canadensis lataxina*
Mountain Lion	*Felis concolor* (released pets?)
Bobcat	*Lynx rufus rufus*
White-tailed Deer	*Odocoileus virginianus borealis*